COOKING WITH **too hot**
tamales

Recipes and Tips from the Television Food Network's Spiciest Cooking Duo

COOKING WITH too hot tamales

mary sue milliken

and susan feniger

WITH HELENE SIEGEL

William Morrow and Company, Inc.
New York

Also by Mary Sue Milliken and Susan Feniger with Helene Siegel

City Cuisine

Mesa Mexicana

Cantina: The Best of Casual Mexican Cooking

It is the policy of William Morrow and Company, Inc., and its imprints and affiliates, recognizing the importance of preserving what has been written, to print the books we publish on acid-free paper, and we exert our best efforts to that end.

Library of Congress Cataloging-in-Publication Data

Milliken, Mary Sue.
Cooking with too hot tamales: recipes and tips from the television food network's spiciest cooking duo / Mary Sue Milliken and Susan Feniger, with Helene Siegel.
p. cm.
Includes index.
ISBN 0-688-15121-3
1. Cookery, Latin American. 2. Cookery, Mexican. 3. Cookery, Spanish.
I. Feniger, Susan. II. Siegel, Helene. III. Title.
TX716.A1M56 1996

641.598—dc20

96-28599
CIP

Printed in the United States of America

First Edition

9 10

BOOK DESIGN BY MICHELE PEREZ

to ruth & ruthie
the too hot moms

acknowledgments

Our warmest thanks to—those who worked tirelessly with immediacy and endurance on the book: Helene Siegel, whose writing is flavorful and straight-forward—just the way we love to cook ■ Michele Perez, whose wise design vision gives this book just the right personality ■ Kathleen Hackett and Ann Bramson, our insightful editors ■ Those at our restaurant, Border Grill, in Santa Monica, who keep the flames flying, especially: Scott Linquist, Martha Wright, Damian Martinez, Doris Chavez, and Carlos Mulia ■ The team at TVFN that consistently makes these tamales sparkle: *Producers:* Julia Harrison and Pat O'Gorman *Kitchen:* Georgia Downard, Susan Stockton, Lauren Deen, Cathy Lowe, Emily Rieger, and Leslie Orlandi *Director:* Dini Diskin-Zimmerman *Researcher:* Jill Abrahams ■ The discerning individuals who developed recipes and show ideas with us: Briget Binns and Joan Nielson ■ Adviser and friend Wendy Glenn, for her perfectly focused guidance in making our dreams come true ■ And to Josh, Liz, and Declan, whose patience and encouragement support us daily, Thank you.

contents

introduction Sharing the Kitchen

Having watched Mary Sue and Susan share a very public kitchen for eight years, since our first collaboration on *City Cuisine,* all I can say is the camera doesn't lie. This is a partnership that really cooks. Let me explain. Just like a marriage, a business partnership is a universe unto itself—one that outsiders often can't comprehend without an experienced tour guide. *C'est moi.* ▪ With Mary Sue and Susan, the language is food and the crucible in which the relationship was first forged was the restaurant kitchen—a place of great pressure and excitement—Jovan Treboyevic's Le Perroquet in Chicago to be exact, where they were the first women in the kitchen. ▪ Both brought along a passion for honing their craft, a capacity for hard work, a drive to go where few women had gone before—to be chef-owners of their own restaurants—and a strong sense of individuality. All of this would be nothing, of course, without terrific stamina, inquisitive appetites, and an ability to rise from the ashes. (Good timing and favorable restaurant reviews haven't hurt either.) ▪ Over fifteen years of opening three restaurants, selling two, collaborating on four cookbooks, one radio show, now a national television show, and traveling the world in search of exciting foods and new ideas, the machine is really humming. Here is how it works—as best I can tell! ▪ *No more food fights:* After spending the first few years quibbling about things like the number of garlic cloves in a stew or how far to brown a roux, they have agreed to disagree. In general, whoever feels the strongest wins, and an unwritten code exists where passion is the final arbiter. (In other words, if your mouth is on fire from

chiles, Susan won.) ▪ *Partners in business, not in life:* They may cook together on television, be partners in a restaurant, sign the same checks, and have an enduring friendship—but that does not mean they are One. Each has a full and demanding personal life apart from work that creates the balance necessary to get back into that kitchen and fold just one more tamale. Susan unwinds by paring down and going to the country, preferably to a Third World country if she has the time, and Mary Sue likes to spend free time at home with her family or traveling to exotic spots with interesting foods to taste and cook. ▪ At work, tasks get divided according to talent and preference. Susan loves the hustle of expediting the "line" so orders get cooked correctly and delivered to their tables promptly, while Mary Sue is an expert pastry maker and heads up the research for their work on radio, television, and books. They don't overlap and they don't get in each other's way, so the whole is greater than the parts. ▪ *Two mouths are better than one, or why settle for less:* In much the same way as marriage partners reevaluate and recommit at certain flash points in the relationship, so do successful partners. The most difficult choice for Susan and Mary Sue was the selling of their once hotter-than-hot City restaurant in Los Angeles in 1994. It forced them each to take a step back and reconsider what came next. For Susan, it was the challenge of making the restaurant business work again, as they have done at Border Grill in Santa Monica, and for Mary Sue, it was the ability to pursue teaching through classes, books, radio, and television. ▪ From the time they started cooking together in the tiny City Café in Los Angeles in 1982, they have always been partial to strong flavors and rustic cuisines. Then it was Indian, Thai, and French country cooking. Now it is Latin American and Spanish cuisine, with an emphasis on home cooking. ▪ With each culture, a new world of spices and native cooking techniques opens up for them to explore—mysterious achiote paste, dried chiles, and epazote in Mexico, fragrant saffron, ground almonds, and vinegary escabeches in Spain, sweet banana leaves and corn husks for wrapping in the other Latin countries. As their palates expand, so do their horizons, keeping those inquisitive taste buds alive and growing and the partnership vibrant. This is, after all, about satisfying appetite. ▪ As in any sane marriage, the option of divorce has been known to pop into each partner's mind as a method of moving one's own program forward. ▪ But time and again, each has come to the conclusion that it is better to have someone to share the ups and downs with, someone to complain to, learn from, and travel with, someone to laugh and share drinks with, and to ponder the wonders of some exotic cuisine with, than to sit in the stew alone. In other words, more is better than less. ▪ And so they continue to cook as one. Luckily for us.

—Helene Siegel

COOKING WITH too hot
tamales

cocktail hour

We are always amazed at the difference a well-planned cocktail hour makes in setting the mood for an evening's festivities. Since most people arrive hungry—and perhaps a bit uneasy about a new situation—this is the prime opportunity for the crafty cook to dazzle guests with small bites of spicy, strong foods and an interesting drink—or two, if you are Mary Sue. If nothing else, guests can always chat about the strange new foods they are tasting, tangle over the guacamole, or clink together ice-cold shots of chile tequila. ■ We prefer to cook as much as possible in advance so we can be out there enjoying the party rather than fussing in the kitchen. In general, we allow about an hour for drinks before dinner and plan to serve four to six bites per person. We strive for a balance between easy and difficult dishes, as well as a balance of flavors, textures, and temperatures. None of this needs to be complicated. If you decide to try the Empanaditas or warm Quinoa Fritters, make the other dish you offer an easy one like Spicy Nut and Raisin Mix or Lemony Mushroom Caps—both of which can be made well in advance. ■ As experienced party givers, we devote as much thought to the beverage selection as to the food. Once again, something a little bit different tweaks everyone's senses and helps the party move forward. For a truly knockout presentation, place the bottle of Chile Tequila in an empty half-gallon milk carton, fill the container with water and some sprigs of cilantro, and freeze. For the party, peel away the cardboard container and display the ice-blocked tequila prominently—it just might get a conversation going. And be sure to try the Mexican version of eggnog—Rompope!

snacks

marinated olives

2 pounds green olives with
 pits, packed in brine

6 tablespoons coriander seeds

¼ cup dried Mexican oregano

10 garlic cloves, thinly sliced

extra virgin olive oil

Serve these special spiced olives with toasted almonds and a nice chilled bottle of fino sherry.

Drain the olives and thoroughly rinse with cold water. Split open with the side of a heavy chef's knife, being careful not to crack the pits.

Place a layer of olives in the bottom of a 1-quart glass jar. Sprinkle with coriander and oregano and scatter a few garlic slices over the top. Repeat the layers until all the olives and spices are used. Add enough olive oil to cover completely. Store in a dark place 2 to 3 weeks, then transfer to the refrigerator. Leftover marinade may be used in a vinaigrette for salad.

Makes 4 cups

spicy nut and raisin mix

2 tablespoons peanut oil

2 garlic cloves, mashed to
   a paste

1 cup golden raisins

²/₃ cup unblanched almonds

²/₃ cup pecans

²/₃ cup unsalted cashew pieces
   or shelled pistachios

2 teaspoons Chile Powder Mix,
   page 134

1 teaspoon cayenne pepper

¹/₂ teaspoon freshly ground
   black pepper

1 tablespoon Worcestershire
   sauce

1¹/₃ cup thin pretzel sticks,
   broken into 1-inch pieces

1 teaspoon coarse salt

pinch of sugar

As restaurateurs, we are always on the lookout for spicy items like this for nibbling with drinks at the bar. Our inspiration here came from that Chex snack that Mary Sue remembers from her mother's bridge parties.

Preheat the oven to 350°F.

Heat the oil in a large cast-iron skillet over medium heat. Sauté the garlic 1 to 2 minutes. Add the raisins, almonds, pecans, cashews, chile powder, cayenne, and black pepper, then add the Worcestershire sauce and mix well. Stir in the pretzels and cook, stirring frequently, 3 to 4 minutes.

Transfer to a baking sheet. Sprinkle with the salt and sugar and bake, shaking the pan and stirring occasionally, 8 to 10 minutes. Turn the mixture into a serving dish and cool.

Makes about 4 cups

tomatillo guacamole in vinegared ancho chiles

4 medium ancho chiles,
   stemmed

2 cups white vinegar

1 cup water

1/2 cup packed brown sugar

1/4 cup olive oil

1 teaspoon coarse salt

1 medium onion, thinly sliced

6 garlic cloves, sliced

5 bay leaves

5 sprigs thyme

1 tablespoon black
   peppercorns

1 teaspoon allspice berries

Tomatillo Guacamole,
   recipe follows

For this festive appetizer, dried ancho chiles are marinated in a vinegary escabeche and then stuffed with a rich, nutty-tasting guacamole. It is a great medley of tastes, textures, and color. For smaller hand-held portions, slice the chiles in half lengthwise and roll each half around a dab of guacamole. Serve with toasted tortilla chips or slices of jícama.

Wash the chiles in warm water. With a paring knife, cut a slit on one side of each and remove and discard the seeds and veins.

Combine the vinegar, water, brown sugar, oil, and salt in a large saucepan. Bring to a boil and cook, stirring occasionally, until the sugar dissolves. Add all the remaining ingredients except the guacamole, reduce to a simmer, and cook about 5 minutes. Remove from the heat.

Stir in the chiles and transfer to a plastic container. Cover and marinate at room temperature 1 day, or store in the refrigerator as long as a week. (Prepare the guacamole just before serving.)

To serve, remove the chiles from the marinade. Stuff with the guacamole and arrange on a serving platter.

Serves 4 to 8

tomatillo guacamole

1 small onion, diced

6 to 8 serrano chiles, stemmed, seeded if desired, and finely chopped

1 bunch cilantro, leaves only, finely chopped

1 teaspoon coarse salt

12 medium tomatillos, husked, washed, and roasted (see below)

$^1/_2$ teaspoon freshly ground black pepper

4 large avocados (about 2 pounds), halved, seeded, and peeled

Combine the onion, chiles, cilantro, and salt in a large bowl. Add the tomatillos, a few at a time, mashing and blending with a fork or pestle to a fine paste. Add the avocados and continue mashing and mixing until chunky. Serve immediately in the ancho chile boats, or as a dip with slices of ripe tomato.

Makes $3^1/_2$ cups

hot tip

HOW TO ROAST TOMATILLOS OR TOMATOES
We prefer to roast tomatillos and tomatoes under the broiler, but when we are in a rush, a hot pan does a fine job. Place the whole fruit, (husk tomatillos first) in a hot skillet or cast-iron griddle over medium-high heat and roast, turning occasionally, until quite charred all over and slightly softened.

chile-toasted coconut strips

1 coconut

1 to 2 tablespoons Chile
    Powder Mix, page 134

1 to 2 teaspoons coarse salt,
    or to taste

juice of 1 lime

Little surprises like these spiced coconut strips, rather than the usual nuts and crackers, signal guests that an interesting meal is set to follow.

Preheat the oven to 325°F.

Poke holes in the three soft areas at the top of the coconut with an icepick or hammer and nail. Drain the milk and save for another use. Place the coconut on a baking sheet and bake 10 minutes, or until the shell and flesh separate. Reduce the oven temperature to 300°F.

Crack open the shell with a hammer. Remove and discard the shell, leaving the brown skin on the coconut meat. Cut the meat into thin strips using a vegetable peeler or the slicing side of a grater. Toss in a bowl with the remaining ingredients.

Arrange the seasoned coconut strips in a single layer on a baking sheet. Toast in the oven 10 to 12 minutes, stirring frequently, until golden brown. Cool and store in an airtight container.

Makes about 4 cups

lemony mushroom caps

1 1/4 pounds small white
   mushroom, stems removed

1 cup olive oil

1/2 cup freshly squeezed
   lemon juice

4 shallots, minced

3 garlic cloves, minced

1 teaspoon cracked black
   pepper

1 bay leaf

1 1/2 teaspoons coarse salt

chopped Italian parsley,
   for garnish

Look for the littlest mushrooms, with tightly closed caps, for marinating. Mary Sue likes to package marinated vegetables like this in glass jars for gift giving at Christmas. They are always terrific to have on hand in the refrigerator when unexpected guests drop in.

Wipe the mushrooms clean with a damp towel. Combine all the remaining ingredients except the parsley in a large bowl and add the mushrooms. Toss to coat evenly. Transfer to a glass or plastic container, pressing the mushrooms down until the liquid rises to the top. Cover tightly and refrigerate 2 to 5 days.

To serve, arrange on a platter and sprinkle with parsley. Serve with toothpicks for spearing.

Makes 1 quart

hot tip

MUSHROOMS AS MEDICINE

We eat mushrooms just because we love them, but it is nice to know of their medicinal qualities. Some, such as shiitakes, are said to be valuable in preventing and treating viral infections. They are also known to lower blood pressure and cholesterol levels and to improve the functioning of the body's immune system.

quinoa
fritters

²/₃ cup quinoa

1 ¹/₃ cups water

¹/₄ cup all-purpose flour

¹/₄ cup grated Cotija,
    Parmesan, or Romano
    cheese

³/₄ teaspoon coarse salt

pinch of freshly ground black
    pepper

4 scallions, white and light
    green parts only, finely
    chopped

¹/₂ bunch Italian parsley,
    leaves only, chopped

1 medium egg

1 egg yolk

³/₄ cup vegetable oil

lemon wedges, for garnish

Red Salsa, page 19, for serving

It is worth the trouble to go to the health food shop for organic quinoa since the flavor is so much better and less bitter than the nonorganic variety that some supermarkets may carry. This dish was inspired by Felipe Rojas-Lombardi, whose cooking we have enjoyed for years.

Wash the quinoa and drain well. Place a small dry saucepan over high heat. Add the quinoa and toast, shaking and stirring constantly with a wooden spoon to prevent scorching, about 5 minutes. Transfer to a large saucepan and add the water. Bring to a boil, reduce to a simmer, and cook, covered, until all the water is absorbed, about 10 minutes. Set aside to cool.

In a large bowl, combine the cooled quinoa, the flour, cheese, salt, and pepper. Add the scallions, parsley, egg, and egg yolk. Blend thoroughly with a wooden spoon until the mixture has the consistency of a soft dough.

Heat the oil in a large skillet over medium heat. Using two soupspoons, press the batter into egg-shaped ovals and gently slide into the hot oil. Fry until the bottoms are golden brown, less than a minute. Turn and fry on the second side until golden, less than a minute. Drain on paper towels and serve warm with lemon wedges and red salsa.

Serves 6

hot tip

PROPER APRON ATTIRE

We recommend plain white full chef's aprons in the kitchen. For efficiency, tie the strings around your waist at the front so you can hang a dish towel at one side of your waist for easy access. This is much easier than those clumsy hot pads, and especially convenient for outdoor grilling.

anchos
huaraches

1 tablespoon lard or
vegetable oil

1 ancho chile, wiped clean,
stemmed, and seeded

1 1/2 teaspoons coarse salt

1/2 teaspoon freshly ground
black pepper

2/3 cup water

1 cup masa harina

1/4 pound panela cheese,
grated

2 tablespoons finely chopped
fresh epazote or oregano

vegetable oil for frying

6 tablespoons grated
Romano cheese

6 tablespoons minced
red onion

Red Salsa, page 19, for dipping

We first tasted these flattened stuffed masa cakes—named after the brown woven sandals—at a Mexico City market, where a street vendor served them topped with a fried egg for breakfast. The smoky red ancho chile permeates the dough with its earthy flavor and color. Huaraches can be made entirely in advance and simply reheated.

Heat the lard in a small skillet over low heat. Sauté the ancho for 1 to 2 minutes, until slightly softened. With a slotted spoon, transfer to a blender, along with 1 teaspoon of the salt, the pepper, and water. Puree until smooth.

In a large bowl, combine the masa with the chile puree. Knead to blend well. To test the consistency, flatten a small ball of dough between your palms. If the edges crack, add water, a tablespoon at a time, until a test piece does not crack. Set aside, covered, at room temperature, for 1 hour for the flavors to develop, or refrigerate up to a week.

Mix together the panela cheese, epazote, and the remaining 1/2 teaspoon salt for the filling.

To stuff, break off tablespoonfuls of the dough and roll between your palms to form small balls. Roll or press each between two sheets of plastic wrap into 4-inch round tortillas. Place 1 tablespoon of the cheese mix on one side of each tortilla. Fold the dough to enclose, then press the edges together to seal. Pat the stuffed tortilla between your palms to flatten evenly to about 1/4 inch thick.

Heat a large cast-iron skillet or griddle over medium heat and lightly coat the bottom with oil. Cook the huaraches 1 to 2 minutes per side, until golden all over. (Huaraches may be made in advance and set aside for the final frying.)

Add about 1½ inches of vegetable oil to a large cast-iron skillet and heat until almost smoking. Fry the huaraches about 30 seconds per side, until lightly browned but not crisp. Drain briefly on paper towels.

Arrange the huaraches on a platter and sprinkle with the Romano cheese and red onion. Serve immediately, with red salsa for dipping. (Finished huaraches may be reheated in a hot oven for 3 to 4 minutes.)

Makes 12 huaraches

hot tip

HOW TO TOAST NUTS

We prefer to toast nuts before adding them to recipes to develop their flavor by bringing their oils to the surface. Simply spread the nuts in a single layer on a baking sheet and toast in a 350°F oven, shaking the pan occasionally for even toasting. Remove when the nuts are golden and fragrant, about ten minutes.

oysters on the half-shell with smoky chipotle vinegar

¹/₃ cup red wine vinegar
(from Pickled Chipotles)

4 shallots, minced

1 Pickled Chipotle, recipe
follows, finely chopped

Coarse salt and freshly ground
black pepper

24 raw oysters in the shell,
scrubbed

Whenever we serve oysters, our goal is to open them fresh, saving as much of their liquor as possible, and to serve them quickly and ice-cold. At the moment we love gorgeous, tiny Fanny Bays and Kuomamotos, but we are always open to new experiences where oysters are concerned. For a quick sauce, try a tiny bit of red or green salsa on fresh oysters—delicious!

Whisk together the vinegar, shallots, and chopped chipotle. Season with salt and pepper.

Shuck the oysters, keeping the rounded bottom shells and discarding the others. Mix up a small bowl of salted water and use a pastry brush to clean off any grit remaining on the inside of the serving shells or on the oysters. Carefully wipe clean the edges of the serving shells. Place one oyster in each and arrange on a serving platter that has been lined with crushed ice sprinkled with coarse salt. Spoon on the chipotle vinegar sparingly and serve.

Serves 2 to 4

pickled chipotles

3 dried chipotle chiles,
    stemmed and seeded if
    desired

1 cup red wine vinegar

Combine the chiles and vinegar in small saucepan. Bring to a boil, reduce to a simmer, and cook, covered, 5 minutes. Set aside to cool. Store in a jar in the refrigerator as long as 6 months.

empanaditas

1 pound lean ground beef

1 medium onion, chopped

2 garlic cloves, minced

$1/2$ cup dark raisins

$1/3$ cup toasted almonds,
coarsely chopped

$1/3$ cup green olives, pitted
and chopped

8 Roma tomatoes, cored
and chopped

2 to 4 serrano chiles, stemmed
and chopped (with seeds)

1 tablespoon ground cumin

$1/2$ teaspoon ground cinnamon

$1/4$ teaspoon ground cloves

1 teaspoon coarse salt

1 teaspoon freshly ground
black pepper

juice of 2 limes

Empanada Dough, recipe
follows

1 egg lightly beaten with
2 tablespoons milk, for
egg wash

Black Jalapeño Salsa,
page 20, for serving
(optional)

The Latin kitchen contains many variations on the savory stuffed pastry packages called empanadas. These tiny, bite-sized, golden-brown bundles are stuffed with a sweet- and-spicy meat filling and then baked rather than fried, for a minimum of fat. Serve with your favorite salsa for dipping.

Brown the ground beef in a large heavy skillet over medium-high heat, stirring frequently, 6 to 8 minutes. Drain off the excess fat. Add the onion and sauté 5 minutes. Add the garlic, raisins, almonds, olives, tomatoes, and chiles. Sauté 2 minutes longer. Stir in the cumin, cinnamon, cloves, salt, and pepper. Cook until the aromas of the spices are released and the pan is nearly dry, about 5 minutes. Stir in the lime juice and set aside to cool.

Meanwhile, roll out the pastry. Divide the dough in half. Roll out on a floured board to a thickness of $1/8$ inch. With a cookie cutter or glass, cut out 3-inch circles. Gather the scraps, add to the remaining dough, and reroll and cut out circles until all the dough is used.

Place a teaspoonful of filling in the center of each pastry round. Fold over and press the edges together to seal. Transfer to a greased baking sheet and chill 30 minutes, or wrap and freeze. (Frozen empanadas need not be defrosted before baking.)

Preheat the oven to 400°F.

Brush the pastries with the egg wash and arrange in a single layer on a baking sheet. Bake until golden, about 15 minutes. Serve hot, with the jalapeño salsa if desired.

Makes about 24 empanaditas

empanada dough

2 cups all-purpose flour

$^1/_2$ teaspoon coarse salt

$^1/_2$ cup lard or vegetable
shortening

$2^1/_2$ tablespoons unsalted
butter

about $^1/_2$ cup ice water

Combine the flour, salt, lard, and butter in a large bowl. Lightly blend with your fingertips until the fat is evenly distributed in chunks. Stir in $^1/_2$ cup ice water.

Turn out onto a floured surface and lightly knead until the dough forms a ball, adding a bit more water if necessary. Wrap in plastic and refrigerate at least 1 hour, or freeze as long as a week. Return to room temperature before rolling.

hot tip

THE IMPORTANCE OF ONIONS

Raw onion is often used in the Latin kitchen as a garnish or key ingredient in ceviches or salsas. To get the proper snap and sparkle, use very fresh onions and chop them as close as possible to the cooking time. It does not take long for chopped onions to lose their sweetness and crunch and become smelly, old onions.

Though there is no surefire way to prevent tears when chopping onions, we have picked up some tricks through the years. First of all, never use the food processor or mini chopper to chop onions—they will be reduced to water and pulp in no time at all. The less chopping the better, so try to use the "three-slice method"—halve the onion and slice first horizontally, then vertically, then across. But to really staunch those tears, try cutting onions near a sink with the water running while whistling at the same time; apparently the molecules that cause tearing are attracted to the wettest thing in the area and so will be drawn to the water rather than your eyes. (Let us know how this works!)

great salsas

fresh salsa

4 medium ripe tomatoes, cored, seeded, and finely diced

¹/₄ red onion, minced

2 jalapeño chiles, stemmed, seeded if desired, and minced

1 bunch cilantro, leaves only, chopped

2 tablespoons freshly squeezed lime juice

³/₄ teaspoon coarse salt

pinch of freshly ground black pepper

Fresh chopped tomato salsa, also known as salsa Mexicana or pico de gallo, is the most popular salsa in and outside of Mexico. We love it with chips, quesadillas, or grilled chicken, fish, or steak. The only trick is to use the freshest ingredients and not to hold it for very long, so the flavors remain fresh.

Combine all of the ingredients in a bowl. Stir and toss well. Serve immediately, or store in a covered container in the refrigerator no longer than a day.

Makes 2 cups; serves 6 as an appetizer with chips

red
salsa

2 tablespoons vegetable oil

1 medium onion, thinly sliced

4 cups diced canned Italian
    plum tomatoes

1 cup tomato juice

2 garlic cloves, peeled

1 large jalapeño chile,
    stemmed and seeded
    if desired

freshly ground black pepper
    to taste

1 teaspoon coarse salt, or
    more to taste

Our basic red sauce for flavoring soups, rice, fideo, chilaquiles, and marinades. If you are looking for an easy sauce to make in bulk and keep in the freezer, this is it.

Heat the oil in a medium skillet over moderate heat. Cook the onion until soft, about 10 minutes. Transfer to a food processor or a blender. Add all the remaining ingredients except the salt, in batches if necessary, and puree until smooth.

Pass through a medium strainer into a bowl, pressing with a wooden spoon or spatula to force through as much pulp as possible. Pour into a saucepan and add the salt. Bring to a boil, reduce to a simmer, and cook, uncovered, 20 minutes. Adjust the seasoning. Set aside to cool for table salsa, or use warm for red rice or chilaquiles. Store in the refrigerator 2 to 3 days or in the freezer for weeks.

Makes 1 quart

black jalapeño salsa

2 ($^1/_2$-inch-thick) slices
   red onion

4 garlic cloves, peeled

2 teaspoons dried Mexican
   oregano

$^1/_4$ cup olive oil

12 jalapeño chiles, stemmed,
   seeded, and halved

3 Anaheim chiles, stemmed,
   seeded, and halved

juice of 2 limes

$^1/_2$ teaspoon coarse salt

If you love chiles as we do, do not miss the opportunity to taste a truly chile-infused sauce. Make it in the summer, when the farmers' market is selling jalapeños by the bagful and you are planning on grilling some steaks. Jalapeños and beef are a natural combination.

Heat a cast-iron skillet over high heat; add the onion slices and char, separating them into rings. Remove from the pan. Toast the garlic until it begins to brown in spots, then add the oregano, cook for a minute, and remove from the pan.

Add the olive oil to the skillet and sear the chiles, turning until evenly charred.

Transfer the chiles, with the onion, garlic, and oregano, to a food processor. Add the remaining ingredients and pulse until finely chopped; for a finer paste, add $^1/_2$ cup water and process until smooth. Store in a plastic container in the refrigerator 2 to 3 days.

Makes about 1$^1/_2$ cups

hot tip

CHILES, CHILES, AND MORE CHILES

It didn't take long for us, especially Susan, to fall in love with chiles, and we suggest you dive right in and get to know them better. Chiles are no more difficult to work with than any other vegetable or fruit and they deliver a great deal of sparkle to your foods for very little cost.

We often specify a range when calling for chiles and sometimes consider the seeds and veins optional. All you really need to know is that most of the heat is stored in the inner membranes, so if what you want is chile flavor without too much heat, scoop out the seeds and veins. (You know what to do if heat is what you are after.) Because a chile's heat will vary according to season, we like to break open a chile and carefully taste it to determine fire power.

Always shop for chiles by appearance rather than name, since that can vary according to the region of the country. Usually, the smaller the chile, the hotter the pepper.

Dried chiles, particular some of our favorites like anchos and chipotles, are available these days at specialty shops and by mail order. Go ahead and buy a bunch once you find a good source. They can be stored, sealed in a plastic bag, in the freezer for a long time.

three-minute salsa

4 Roma tomatoes, cored and
   quartered

1 to 2 serrano chiles,
   stemmed, seeded if desired,
   and sliced

juice of 1 to 2 limes

1 teaspoon coarse salt

$^1\!/_2$ teaspoon freshly ground
   black pepper

This is one of our favorite easy salsas, for dips and chips, topping a quesadilla, or for a quick throw-together sauce for grilled foods.

Combine all of the ingredients in a blender and puree until smooth. Store in a covered container in the refrigerator no longer than a day.

Makes $^3\!/_4$ cup

hot tip
AVOCADOS AND HOW TO PIT THEM
We prefer Hass, the medium-sized pebbly skinned avocado from California and Mexico, for all our cooking because of its rich, nutty flavor. To peel and pit, first cut the fruit in half. Then place on a counter and hit the pit with the sharp edge of the knife so it plunges in. Lift in one hand and twist with the other to remove the pit and knock the knife on the counter to dislodge the pit. Cut in quarters and peel.

chile árbol avocado salsa

1/2 pound Roma tomatoes

3/4 pound tomatillos, husked and washed

1/4 cup (10 to 12) árbol chiles, stemmed

1 bunch cilantro, leaves only, roughly chopped

1 medium onion, chopped

2 tablespoons ground cumin

4 garlic cloves, crushed

2 cups water

1 teaspoon coarse salt

1/2 teaspoon freshly ground black pepper

1 slightly underripe avocado, halved, seeded, peeled, and finely diced

In the kitchen at the Border Grill, we've seen cooks pull this intriguing red and green salsa together even faster by eliminating the roasting. Just be sure to let it cool before stirring in the avocado.

Preheat the broiler.

Place the tomatoes and tomatillos on a foil-lined baking sheet. Broil, turning occasionally, until charred all over, 10 to 12 minutes. Transfer to a saucepan along with all the remaining ingredients except the avocado.

Bring to a boil and cook over medium heat until the onion softens, 12 to 15 minutes. Transfer to a food processor or a blender. Puree and then strain. Store the salsa, without the avocado, in the refrigerator in a covered container up to 5 days, or freeze as long as 4 weeks. Just before serving, stir in the avocado.

Makes 2 1/2 cups

chipotle tomatillo salsa

1 small onion, chopped

2 garlic cloves, peeled

2 dried chipotle chiles

$^1/_2$ bunch cilantro, leaves
   and stems

$^1/_2$ cup water

2 teaspoons coarse salt, or
   to taste

$^1/_2$ to 1 teaspoon sugar, or
   to taste

$^1/_2$ pound tomatillos, husked,
   washed, and roasted
   (see page 7)

juice of 1 lime

This more complex salsa balances spicy smoky chipotles, one of our favorite chiles, with tart tomatillos.

Combine the onion, garlic, chipotles, cilantro, and water in a small saucepan. Bring to a boil and simmer until the chile softens about 5 minutes. Transfer to a blender. Add the remaining ingredients and puree until smooth. Store in a container in the refrigerator 2 to 3 days.

Makes about 1$^1/_2$ cups

green salsa

1 pound tomatillos, husked, washed, and quartered

2 to 4 large jalapeño chiles, stemmed, seeded if desired, and coarsely chopped

$^1\!/_2$ cup cold water

$^1\!/_2$ medium onion, halved

2 bunches cilantro, stems and leaves

2 teaspoons coarse salt

Tomatillos are used in the Mexican kitchen to cut the richness of more complicated dishes. Tomatillos are not green tomatoes at all as many people think; they are a relative of the Cape gooseberry and a member of the nightshade family. Their flavor is tart and acidic.

Place the tomatillos, jalapeños, and water in a blender or a food processor and puree just until chunky. Add the remaining ingredients and puree about 2 minutes more, or until smooth. Store in the refrigerator, in a sealed container, up to 3 days.

Makes $3^1\!/_2$ cups

cocktails (with and without the booze)

The gathering immediately feels more festive when you serve guests a beautiful, made-from-scratch beverage like fruit punch or sangría. We've included a number of juice-based drinks, with and without alcohol, and, of course, the mixed tequila drinks Border Grill is famous for. All mirror the colorful spirit of Mexico and carry Mary Sue's personal seal of approval.

refresco de mango

4 cups cubed ripe mango

3 cups water

$^1/_4$ cup sugar, or to taste

juice of 1 lemon, or to taste

lime wedges, for garnish

float of tequila (optional)

In a blender, combine the mango and water and puree until smooth. Thin with more water if desired, and add the sugar and lemon juice. Blend again and serve in tall glasses, over ice, with a thin layer of tequila if desired, and wedges of lime.

Serves 4 to 6

minty lime cooler

1/2 cup freshly squeezed lime juice

1/3 cup sugar

1/2 cup packed fresh mint leaves

1 (12-ounce) bottle sparkling water, chilled

lime slices, for garnish

mint sprigs, for garnish

Combine the lime juice, sugar, and mint in a blender. Puree until smooth. Fill two tall glasses half-full with ice cubes. Pour half of the lime juice concentrate into each. Top with the sparkling water, garnish with lime and mint, and serve.

Serves 2

hot tip

HOW TO JUICE A LIME OR LEMON

Limes in particular often contain very little juice. To wring the most from your limes, first roll them back and forth on the counter, bearing down with your full weight to break up and loosen the juice pods. Cut in half, pierce with a fork, and twist both wrists to extract the juice.

chile
tequila

1 (750-milliliter) bottle tequila

2 medium ancho chiles,
    wiped clean

2 jalapeño chiles, washed
    and thoroughly dried

In the original bottle or in a decorative bottle, combine the tequila and chiles. Cap tightly and let sit in a dark place 7 to 10 days to infuse. Replace the original cap with a screened liquor spout (available from bar suppliers) and use for martinis or other cocktails. After 10 days, you may want to strain out the chiles, since their heat increases over time.

Makes about 3 cups

tequila
martini

2 ounces tequila, preferably
    aged blue agave

4 ice cubes

$^{1}/_{2}$ teaspoon Triple Sec

twist of lime

thin strip of serrano chile

In a pitcher or cocktail shaker, combine the tequila and ice and stir or shake 20 times. Pour the Triple Sec into a chilled cocktail glass, swirl to coat the bottom and sides, and pour off. Strain the tequila into the glass. Thread the lime twist and chile strip onto a cocktail skewer, perch on the rim of the glass, and serve.

Serves 1

mexicano cocktail

1 (1 ½-pound) yellow watermelon, peeled, seeded, and
   cut into chunks

¾ cup aged blue agave tequila

6 ice cubes, crushed

1 cup water, or to taste

6 sprigs fresh mint, for garnish

6 small spears red
   watermelon, for garnish
   (optional)

In a blender, combine the watermelon chunks, tequila, ice, and water. Blend until smooth and immediately pour into chilled wine glasses. Garnish each with a sprig of mint and a red watermelon spear.

Serves 6

fresh fruit punch

2 cups sugar

1 cup water

1 (750-milliliter) bottle dry
   white wine

1 (1.5-liter) bottle sparkling
   water

6 cups chopped seeded
   watermelon

1 cup chopped mango
   or papaya

1 cup chopped pineapple

Combine the sugar and water in a saucepan. Bring to a boil and simmer, stirring occasionally, until the sugar is dissolved and the syrup is clear. Set aside to cool.

Combine the syrup, wine, and sparkling water in a pitcher or punch bowl and stir well. Add the fruit. Serve ice cold.

Serves 12 to 16

spiced red sangría

2 cinnamon sticks, cracked

6 whole cloves

6 black peppercorns, cracked

3 allspice berries

1 cup water

$^1\!/_2$ cup sugar

4 oranges

1 lemon

1 lime

1 (750-millileter) bottle light, fruity red wine

2 cups ice cubes

Place the cinnamon, cloves, peppercorns, and allspice in a small saucepan with water and sugar and stir to dissolve. Bring to boil, reduce heat, and simmer for 2 minutes. Turn off the heat and let cool to room temperature, then strain and discard the spices.

Cut 1 of the oranges, the lemon, and the lime into $^1\!/_4$-inch slices.

Juice the remaining 3 oranges. Place the orange juice, sliced fruit, syrup, and wine into a pitcher filled with ice. Stir briskly and serve.

Serves 4

bubbly white sangría

½ pound seedless green
grapes, stemmed

1 to 2 Red Delicious apples,
cored and thinly sliced

1 (750-milliliter) bottle fruity
white wine

1 cup passion fruit or
mango nectar

1 cup pineapple juice

2 cups sparkling water

2 cups ice cubes

Combine the grapes, apples, and wine in a pitcher and let sit, refrigerated, 1 to 2 hours. Pour in the fruit juices, and sparkling water, add the ice cubes, and serve.

Serves 4

tequila con sangrita

2 1/4 cups freshly squeezed
orange juice

3/4 cup freshly squeezed
lime juice

5 tablespoons grenadine syrup

1 generous teaspoon coarse
salt

1 teaspoon cayenne pepper

tequila

Combine all of the ingredients except the tequila in a blender and puree until frothy; or whisk together in a bowl. Pour into a pitcher and chill. Serve cold in shot glasses, with shots of tequila.

Makes 18 shots

rompope

8¹/₂ cups milk

2 cups sugar

2 small cinnamon sticks

6 large egg yolks

1 cup brandy

Great for egg nog lovers who stay away from raw eggs.

Combine 8 cups of the milk, the sugar, and cinnamon in a saucepan and bring to a boil. Simmer, stirring occasionally, 15 minutes.

In a bowl, whisk together the egg yolks with the remaining ½ cup milk. Slowly whisk some of the hot milk into the yolks, then add to the pot with the simmering milk and cook, stirring frequently, until the mixture reaches the consistency of a thin sauce, about 10 minutes. Stir in the brandy and remove from the heat. Let cool, pour into a pitcher, and chill. Serve over ice with a dusting of cinnamon.

Serves 8 to 10

little treasures

Here are the show-off dishes, designed to impress guests and provide busy work for those whose idea of weekend relaxation is hunkering down with a good, if labor-intensive, recipe. For us, tamales are the ultimate portable party food. We like to make them with a group, so all that folding and tying can be shared, and then take them to parties—so everyone can get his or her own little gift to unwrap. Foods cooked in wrappers have an extra layer of flavor we adore. They pick up the flavor of the wrapper itself (corn for tamales), which in turn creates a seal that intensifies all the flavors in the package. Much of the inspiration for these little treasures comes from the Mexican tradition of *antojitos,* or cornmeal-based snacks, and Spanish *tapas*—both hearty little bites that make delicious small meals for less-structured occasions.

escalivada

3 medium tomatoes, halved
   crosswise

15 garlic cloves (unpeeled)

1 ½ pounds Japanese eggplant

3 large red bell peppers

3 medium onions, peeled

⅓ cup Spanish olive oil

1 teaspoon coarse salt

½ teaspoon freshly ground
   black pepper

juice of 1 lemon

½ bunch Italian parsley,
   leaves only, chopped

⅓ cup crumbled goat cheese
   (optional)

⅓ cup Spanish pimiento-
   stuffed green olives,
   coarsely chopped

1 loaf white country bread,
   sliced ½ inch thick and
   toasted, for serving

Escalivada, a popular Spanish dish of roasted and marinated vegetables, is a great do-ahead starter to serve in place of salad. Roasting at a low temperature intensifies and sweetens the flavor of vegetables beautifully.

Preheat the oven to 350°F.

Rub the vegetables with half of the olive oil. Arrange on a baking sheet, placing the tomatoes cut side up and tucking the garlic under the vegetables. Roast until softened and golden, removing the tomatoes after about 15 minutes, the garlic after 30 minutes and the eggplant, peppers, and onions after 45 minutes to 1 hour. Set aside to cool.

Peel the garlic and halve the cloves lengthwise. Peel the eggplant and peppers and tear into thin strips. Peel the softened onions, cut into slices, and separate rings. (The pieces should be small enough to be scooped easily onto a slice of bread.)

Arrange the vegetables on a large platter, making an attractive pattern with the colors. Season with the salt and pepper and sprinkle with the lemon juice. Drizzle with the remaining oil and sprinkle with the parsley. Dot with the goat cheese if desired and scatter the olives over the top. Serve family style, with a basket of the freshly toasted bread.

Serves 6

cactus
tacos

1 $\frac{1}{2}$ pounds fresh or 1 pound
   prepared cactus paddles
   (nopales), needles removed

$\frac{3}{4}$ cup olive oil

1 $\frac{1}{2}$ teaspoons coarse salt

1 $\frac{1}{2}$ teaspoons freshly ground
   black pepper

4 Roma tomatoes, cored,
   seeded, and diced

$\frac{1}{2}$ small red onion, diced

1 to 2 medium serrano chiles,
   stemmed, seeded, and finely
   diced

2 bunches cilantro, leaves only,
   chopped

$\frac{1}{2}$ cup finely grated Cotija,
   añejo, or Parmesan cheese

$\frac{1}{2}$ cup red wine vinegar

20 Corn Tortillas, page 55,
   toasted

lettuce leaves, for garnish

avocado slices, for garnish

cracked black pepper

We are continually amazed at what a popular choice this cactus salad is at the restaurant. These tacos make a great little meal for the adventurous vegetarian.

Preheat the grill or broiler.

Place the cactus paddles in a bowl and toss with $\frac{1}{4}$ cup of the olive oil and $\frac{1}{2}$ teaspoon each of the salt and pepper. Grill or broil the paddles, turning once, until grill marks appear, or they turn dark green with black patches, 3 to 5 minutes. Set aside to cool to room temperature. Cover and chill 2 hours, or overnight.

Cut the cactus into $\frac{1}{2}$-inch pieces. In a large bowl, combine the cactus, tomatoes, onion, chiles, cilantro, and cheese. Add the remaining $\frac{1}{2}$ cup olive oil, the vinegar, and the remaining 1 teaspoon each salt and pepper. Toss well.

To serve, stack 2 warmed tortillas for each taco. Top each with a lettuce leaf, some of the cactus salad mix, and a slice of avocado. Sprinkle with cracked pepper and serve.

Serves 10

fresh corn tamales with roasted red peppers

10 ears corn (or use 3 cups good-quality thawed frozen or canned corn, with 1 [8-ounce] package dried corn husks, softened as on page 46)

2 tablespoons unsalted butter

$1/2$ cup dried hominy grits

1 teaspoon paprika

$1/2$ cup diced roasted red bell pepper

$1/2$ teaspoon coarse salt

$1/4$ teaspoon white pepper

pinch of sugar (optional)

$1/2$ cup heavy cream

$1/2$ teaspoon baking powder

Fresh Salsa, page 18, for serving

sour cream, for serving

Our reputation as tamale makers was made at the original Border Grill with these sweet, creamy corn tamales. We have cooked and tasted many since, but few are as delicious and easy to make. If fresh corn is not in season, frozen corn and dried husks are good alternatives.

Remove the corn husks by cutting off both ends of the cobs, trying to keep the husks whole. Place the largest husks in a pot of hot water and set aside to soak.

To make the stuffing, working over a bowl, run the point of a sharp knife down the center of each row of kernels to release the juices, and then scrape with the dull side to remove the kernels from the cob.

Melt the butter in a large skillet over medium heat. Sauté the grits with the paprika 1 to 2 minutes. Add the red pepper, the corn and its juices, the salt, white pepper, sugar to taste, and the cream and simmer until the mixture thickens, 5 to 8 minutes. Set aside to cool. Then stir in the baking powder and refrigerate.

Drain the corn husks on paper towels. Make ties for the tamales by cutting a few of the husks into 10 to 12 strips.

To stuff the tamales, overlap 2 or 3 husks on a counter and spread about 3 tablespoons of filling down the center. Fold over the sides and then the ends to enclose the filling. Tie with a corn husk string. Repeat with the remaining husks and filling.

In a steamer or large pot fitted with a rack, make a bed for the tamales by lining the steamer rack with the remaining corn husks. Add the tamales and steam over low heat 1 hour.

Remove from the steamer and let rest 10 minutes. Serve hot with the fresh salsa and sour cream. (Leftover tamales can be reheated in a steamer over simmering water for 20 to 30 minutes.)

Makes 10 to 12 tamales; serves 6

hot tip

THE IMPORTANCE OF SALT

Salt is probably the most important ingredient in the kitchen, and yet it is often overlooked or considered an afterthought. We like to keep it in a bowl near the stove for easy sprinkling as we cook and on the table as well, for guests to add to taste. We use kosher salt in the kitchen for its pure, mild flavor but we suggest sampling some of the many varieties on today's market: red clay salt from Hawaii, sea salts from all over the world, and English flake salt, to name a few.

stacked enchiladas de manchego

Chile Sauce

30 dried red chiles, such as
New Mexican, pasilla or
guajillo

3 cups water

1 onion, quartered

3 garlic cloves, minced

1 tablespoon dried oregano,
crumbled

$1^{1}/_{2}$ teaspoons ground cumin

1 teaspoon sugar

1 teaspoon coarse salt

pinch of freshly ground
black pepper

2 tablespoons olive oil

Enchiladas

$1^{1}/_{4}$ pounds Mexican
Manchego or Monterey Jack
cheese, grated

1 medium onion, diced

8 jalapeño chiles, stemmed
and thinly sliced

1 bunch cilantro, leaves only,
chopped

Enchiladas are one of those simple foods like Italian lasagne that grew bigger, heavier, and just plain cheesier as they were adapted by American cooks. Here we return to the original Mexican concept of a simple stack of layered fresh tortillas, chile sauce, and a smattering of cheese. These make a lovely weeknight supper.

To make the sauce, wash the chiles and remove their stems, seeds, and veins. Bring the water to a boil in a medium saucepan and add the chiles. Cover and remove from the heat. Let stand 1 hour, or until softened. Drain, reserving the soaking water.

Combine the chiles and 2 cups of their soaking water in a blender with the onion, garlic, oregano, cumin, sugar, salt, and pepper. Puree until smooth, adding a bit more of the reserved water if necessary.

Heat the olive oil in a large skillet over medium-low heat. Pour in the chile sauce and cook, stirring occasionally, until slightly thickened, about 10 minutes. Adjust the seasonings, remove from the heat, and cover to keep warm.

To make the enchiladas, combine the Manchego cheese, onion, jalapeños, and cilantro in a bowl; toss well.

In large skillet, heat 1 inch of oil over medium-high heat. Fry the tortillas, one at a time, about 30 seconds, or until slightly golden but still pliable. Drain on paper towels.

Preheat the oven to 300°F.

canola or vegetable oil, for
frying

24 Corn Tortillas, page 55

1 cup crumbled panela or
farmer's cheese

cilantro sprigs, for garnish

Dip a tortilla in the pan of sauce to coat lightly and then place on a large baking sheet. Scatter about 2 tablespoons of the cheese mixture over the tortilla. Dip another tortilla, place it over the first, and top with more cheese. Repeat with 2 more tortillas. Then repeat the procedure until all of the tortillas have been layered into 6 stacks. Transfer to the oven to warm through and melt the cheese.

To serve, lightly coat six dinner plates with chile sauce. With a spatula, transfer the stacks to the plates. Top each with a little more sauce, some of the crumbled panela and a few sprigs of cilantro. Serve immediately.

Serves 6

hot tip

THE GOOD SPANISH STUFF

On our trips to Spain, we have discovered some wonderful products that are now an everyday part of our kitchen. Spanish olive oil and sherry vinegar are much less expensive than comparable Italian products and they are just as good or better. Other favorites are cheeses like Manchego and Cabrales, a blue cheese, pimientos, anchovies, and quince paste.

pickled shrimps

1 pound large shrimp, peeled
   and deveined

coarse salt and freshly ground
   black pepper

$^1/_3$ cup olive oil

2 small onions, thinly sliced

6 jalapeño chiles, stemmed
   and thinly sliced

4 garlic cloves, crushed

1 tablespoon paprika

1 teaspoon ground cumin

$^1/_4$ teaspoon grated nutmeg

2 bay leaves

1 cup white vinegar

Garnishes

mixed baby lettuce leaves

8 radishes, sliced

16 green olives, pitted and
   sliced

A strong, vinegary escabeche like this one needs a firm fish like shrimp to stand up to it without being overwhelmed. Escabeches are a good choice for entertaining, since they can marinate for a day or two in the refrigerator.

Season the shrimp all over with 1 teaspoon salt and $^1/_2$ teaspoon pepper. Heat 1 tablespoon of the olive oil in a large skillet over high heat. Sauté the shrimp, in two batches, until lightly browned, about 3 to 4 minutes. With a slotted spoon, transfer to a plastic or glass container.

Add the remaining oil and all the remaining ingredients except the garnishes to the skillet. Season to taste with salt and pepper. Bring to a boil, reduce to a simmer, and cook until the onions are tender, about 5 minutes.

Pour the vinegar mixture over the shrimp. Cover and chill overnight. Serve on baby lettuce leaves, and garnish with the radishes and green olives.

Serves 4 to 6

shrimp ceviche verde

1 pound rock shrimp

$^{1}/_{2}$ cup freshly squeezed
   lime juice

1 teaspoon coarse salt

$^{1}/_{2}$ teaspoon freshly ground
   black pepper

1 small avocado, halved,
   seeded, peeled, and diced

1 garlic clove, minced

1 teaspoon sugar

6 tomatillos, husked, washed,
   and cut into $^{1}/_{4}$-inch dice

4 jalapeño chiles, stemmed,
   seeded, and chopped

1 bunch scallions, thinly sliced

1 bunch cilantro, leaves only,
   chopped

When we started exploring the Mexican kitchen, we immediately fell in love with the wide variety of ceviches, the marinated raw fish dishes. This is a great one for the home cook since the fish is quickly precooked (rock shrimp is widely available frozen and vacuum-packed) and the flavors are very fresh yet mellowed by the avocados.

Bring a large pot of salted water to a boil. Add the shrimp, return to a boil, cover, turn off heat and let sit 1 to 3 minutes. Drain.

In a glass or ceramic bowl, toss together the shrimp, lime juice, salt, and pepper. Marinate in the refrigerator 1 hour.

Drain the shrimp, reserving the lime juice.

In another glass or ceramic bowl, combine the shrimp with the remaining ingredients. Toss until creamy, then add the reserved lime juice to taste. Serve, or store in the refrigerator.

Serves 4 to 6

hot tip

STORING CILANTRO

Fresh cilantro is so delicate it is hard to keep for very long. We like to store it with roots (or stems) in a glass of water in the refrigerator. Cover the tops loosely with a plastic bag.

wrapped spicy snapper

1 (8-ounce) package dried
corn husks

4 ancho chiles, wiped clean,
lightly toasted (see page
105), stemmed, and seeded

^{1}/$_2$ cup white vinegar

^{1}/$_2$ cup warm water

1 tablespoon cumin seeds

2 teaspoons dried oregano,
crumbled

2 teaspoons dried thyme,
crumbled

2 teaspoons coarse salt

1 teaspoon freshly ground
black pepper

4 garlic cloves, peeled

2 tablespoons olive oil

1^1/$_2$ pounds skinless whitefish
fillets, such as snapper or
sea bass

Garnishes

1 small onion, finely chopped

^{1}/$_2$ bunch cilantro, leaves only,
finely chopped

2 serrano chiles, stemmed,
seeded, and thinly sliced

2 limes, quartered

Wrapped foods are an excellent choice for dinner parties since they add an immediate element of fun. Wrapping the fish in corn husks before grilling seals in all of the juices and seasonings so that the fish steams in the fragrant liquid. While the fire is still hot, wrap some corn tortillas in foil and heat through on the grill to serve with the fish.

Place the corn husks in a saucepan with enough water to cover. Tamp down the husks with a plate to completely submerge them and simmer about 10 minutes. Remove from the heat and let stand, in the water, a few hours, until pliable.

Meanwhile, place the toasted anchos in a bowl. Add the vinegar and warm water and soak about 20 minutes. Drain, reserving the soaking liquid, and transfer to a blender. Add the cumin, oregano, thyme, salt, pepper, garlic, and olive oil. Puree, adding just enough of the soaking liquid to make a smooth paste.

Cut the fish into 3 × 1-inch pieces. Place in a glass or ceramic bowl, add the ancho chile paste, and toss to coat evenly. Cover and refrigerate 30 minutes to 1 hour.

Choose enough of the largest and most pliable corn husks, patching them together as necessary, to make 12 sheets for wrapping the fish. Drain the corn husks on paper towels. Make 6 ties by tearing a few of the remaining husks into strips. Divide the fish into 6 portions.

Arrange 6 corn husk sheets on a work counter. Place a portion of fish on the wider end of each. Fold over the sides and then the ends to enclose. Lay the wrapped fish seam side down on top of a second corn husk sheet and wrap again to enclose thoroughly. Tie each packet twice around the width with a husk strip to seal. The wrapped fish may be held in the refrigerator until ready to cook.

Preheat the grill or heat a large griddle over medium-high heat. Place the packets on the grill or griddle and cook, turning frequently, about 12 minutes, or until the husks start to dry out and color a bit. Open one to check for doneness.

To serve, cut the ties and carefully unwrap and remove the outer layer of husks. Set each on a serving plate, and carefully open the remaining husks. Pass the onion, cilantro, chiles, and limes.

Serves 6

grilled halibut and white bean burritos

²/₃ cup lard or ¹/₃ cup unsalted
   butter and ¹/₃ cup olive oil

1 large onion, diced

2 large garlic cloves, minced

coarse salt and freshly ground
   black pepper

2 cups cooked white beans,
   mashed

2 Roma tomatoes, cored, peeled,
   seeded, and diced

¹/₂ small bunch fresh thyme,
   leaves only, chopped

olive oil for coating

³/₄ pound thick halibut or other
   firm whitefish fillets

4 large Flour Tortillas, page 56,
   toasted

1 cup Green Salsa, page 25

1 avocado, halved, seeded,
   peeled, and sliced

2 large tomatoes, cored and sliced

2 small bunches watercress,
   coarse stems removed, washed
   and dried, or 1 small head
   lettuce, separated into leaves,
   washed, and dried

2 tablespoons freshly squeezed
   lime juice

2 tablespoons olive oil

¹/₄ pound feta cheese, crumbled

White beans and halibut bring this dish just about as far from Mexico as it can go and still be a burrito. The flavors are favorites of ours from the Mediterranean and the mixed salad is our way of lightening a traditionally heavy dish. But the proof is in the tasting—these are fantastic.

Heat the lard in a medium saucepan over medium-high heat. Sauté the onion until golden, 5 to 7 minutes. Add the garlic, 1 teaspoon salt, and ¹/₂ teaspoon pepper, reduce the heat to medium-low, and cook about 2 minutes. Stir in the beans and cook, stirring occasionally, until all the liquid evaporates and the beans form a mass that pulls away from the sides of the pan. Stir in the tomatoes and thyme and set aside.

Preheat the grill or heat a large griddle pan over medium-high heat and lightly coat with oil. Grill the fish just until firm, about 4 minutes per side. Transfer to a board and cut into ¹/₂-inch chunks. Divide into 4 portions.

To fill the burritos, lay the warm tortillas on a counter. Divide the bean mixture into 4 portions and spread in a strip down the center of each tortilla. Top each with a portion of fish and a few spoonfuls of salsa. Combine the remaining ingredients in a bowl, add salt and pepper to taste, and lightly toss. Top the fish with the salad. Fold up the bottom quarter of each tortilla and then roll from one side into a cylinder. Serve seam side down.

Serves 4

striped bass en escabeche

6 fillets striped bass (about
   3 pounds)

2 teaspoons coarse salt

5 tablespoons olive oil

1 teaspoon black peppercorns

1 teaspoon coriander seeds

1 teaspoon cumin seeds

1 taspoon dried oregano,
   toasted (see page 109)

$1/4$ teaspoon ground cinnamon

2 allspice berries

2 whole cloves

2 small bay leaves

10 small garlic cloves, sliced

1 teaspoon sugar

1 cup red wine vinegar

$1/2$ cup water

Corn Tortillas, page 55,
   toasted, or toasted country
   bread, for serving

4 avocados, halved, peeled,
   mashed, and seasoned, for
   serving (optional)

The vinegar and spice dressing called escabeche makes a refreshing marinade for lightly cooked fish. Serve on beds of shredded lettuce for a formal first course or on a platter with crackers and toasts for a buffet.

Pat the fish dry and season all over with salt. Heat 1 tablespoon of the olive oil in a large skillet over high heat. Sear the fish 1 to 2 minutes per side. Transfer to a platter. Cover with plastic wrap and set aside.

Combine the salt, peppercorns, coriander, cumin, oregano, cinnamon, allspice, and cloves in a mini processor or mortar and pestle and finely grind.

Transfer the spice mixture to a saucepan and add the remaining ingredients, including the remaining $1/4$ cup olive oil. Bring to a boil. Cook 5 minutes, and immediately pour over fish fillets. Cover and marinate 2 hours at room temperature or as long as overnight in the refrigerator (bring to room temperature before serving).

To serve, flake the fish and return to the escabeche mixture. Serve with warm tortillas or toasted country bread, and mashed avocado if desired.

Serves 10

hot tip

THE ONION AND GARLIC COMBINATION

To prevent burning when sautéing onion and garlic
together, we like to start by cooking the onion. Then,
when it has softened or colored, we add the garlic and
sauté just for a brief moment, to release its aroma before
adding the next ingredients. This method results in a
fresher garlic flavor and few or no burnt bits.

turkey
tacos

1/2 pound boneless turkey
   breast

1 tablespoon olive oil

coarse salt and freshly ground
   black pepper

4 Corn Tortillas, page 55,
   toasted

1 can (10 ounces) refried black
   beans, warmed

about 2 tablespoons Red
   Salsa, page 19

Pickled Shallots, page 79,
   for garnish

avocado slices, for garnish

Thinly sliced turkey, well seasoned and pan-seared, makes an excellent, quick taco filling. These tacos actually bear more resemblance to authentic Mexican food than all those crisp ground beef tacos.

Slice the turkey into thin scallops. Cover with plastic wrap and pound to flatten slightly. In a medium bowl, combine the turkey with the oil and salt and pepper to taste, and toss to coat.

Preheat the grill or heat a dry cast-iron pan over high heat until smoking. Sear the turkey about 30 seconds per side. Transfer to a cutting board. Cut into 1/2-inch strips and transfer to a bowl, with any juices from the board.

To make the tacos, stack 2 of the warm tortillas. Spread with half the black beans and top with half the seared turkey, a tablespoon each of salsa and pickled shallots, and a few avocado slices. Repeat to make another taco, and serve hot.

Serves 2

turkey tamales with fresh cranberry salsa

1 (8-ounce) package dried
    corn husks

Turkey Braised in Black Mole,
    page 106, turkey meat
    combined with enough
    sauce to cover and extra
    sauce reserved for serving

1 cup chicken stock

1 teaspoon baking soda

2 1/2 teaspoons coarse salt

1 1/2 pounds ground masa for
    tamales, chilled

1/2 cup lard or vegetable
    shortening, chilled

4 poblano chiles, roasted,
    peeled, and seeded

Fresh Cranberry Salsa,
    recipe follows, for serving

Tamales like these, with their rich mole and homemade masa, are meant to be party food and are traditionally made at holiday time by a group of cooks so the tasks can be shared. These would be great at Thanksgiving.

The fresh cranberry relish is not only a new twist, it represents another culinary turnaround for Mary Sue, who detested the astringency of raw cranberries until she came to love this salsa. Now she refuses to eat her turkey and gravy without it.

Place the dried corn husks in a saucepan with water to cover and simmer about 10 minutes. Remove from the heat, weight with a plate to keep the husks submerged, and soak 2 hours, or overnight, until completely flexible. Mix together 1/2 cup of the mole sauce, the chicken stock, baking soda, and salt. Set aside.

Place the masa in the bowl of an electric mixer and beat at medium speed until light in texture, 5 to 7 minutes. Slowly add the chicken stock mixture, beating continuously at medium-high speed. Turn the mixer speed up to high and add the lard a tablespoon at a time, beating well after each addition. Continue beating and scraping down the bowl until the mixture is light and fluffy, about 15 minutes total. Test for lightness by dropping 1 tablespoon of the masa mixture into cold water: If it floats, the mixture is light enough; if not, beat at high speed a few minutes longer.

To make the tamales, spread 1 large or 2 small corn husks on a counter, with the narrow end pointing away from you. Leaving 2 inches bare at the top, spread about 2 1/2 table-spoons of the masa mixture over the center and one side of the husk. Top with a spoonful of the turkey mole. Fold the side covered with masa over to enclose the mole and fold over the bare side of the husk. Fold the top down and place on a square of foil. Wrap to enclose. Repeat with remaining ingredients.

To cook, line a steamer or a rack fitted into a large pot with corn husks and add the tamales. Steam over simmering water 1¼ hours, or until the husks just pull away from the masa without sticking. Serve hot with a tablespoon of the mole sauce and a teaspoonful of cranberry salsa atop each opened tamale.

Makes 12 to 14 tamales; serves 12 as an appetizer, 6 as an entrée

hot tip

COOKING WITH DRIED SPICES

To get the best results from dried spices, cook them first in fat, as you would onion or garlic at the beginning of a dish, to release their oils and thus spread their flavors evenly throughout the dish. If a finished soup or stew needs more flavor, just heat some oil in a small pan, briefly fry additional spices, and stir in. Frying the spices adds a deeper flavor than just tossing them into boiling liquid at the end of cooking, when the flavors do not have a chance to develop.

fresh cranberry salsa

1 pound fresh or thawed
   frozen cranberries

1 cup sugar

2 teaspoons grated
   orange zest

3 Granny Smith apples,
   peeled and diced

3 oranges, peeled, seeded,
   and diced

4 serrano chiles, stemmed
   and diced (with seeds)

1 bunch cilantro, leaves
   and stems, chopped

1 bunch scallions, chopped

Finely chop the cranberries in a food processor or by hand. Combine in a bowl with the remaining ingredients and mix together. Set aside at room temperature 1 hour and then chill until ready to serve. Store in the refrigerator as long as 3 days.

Makes about 3 cups

corn tortillas

4 cups finely ground deep yellow masa harina, or white masa harina

2 ³/₄ cups water

1 teaspoon coarse salt

We recommend making homemade tortillas at least once so you have a yardstick against which to measure factory-made ones. We use a deep yellow masa harina made by Aztec Milling Co. in Los Angeles, which is worth the search if you can find it. These are deep yellow in color, pebbly in texture, and permeated with the unmistakable flavor of sweet, earthy corn. The white masa harina widely available from Quaker makes a respectable tortilla well worth the effort, too.

Combine the masa harina, water, and salt in a large bowl and stir until smooth. The dough should be slightly sticky and form a ball when pressed together. To test, flatten a small ball of dough between your palms. If the edges crack, add water, a tablespoon at a time, until a test piece does not crack.

Divide the dough into 24 small balls for tacos or 12 large balls for quesadillas. Place on a platter and cover with a damp towel.

Line a tortilla press with 2 sheets of heavy plastic (we use a heavy duty freezer bag).

Heat a dry cast-iron skillet or nonstick pan until moderately hot. Flatten each ball of dough in the tortilla press, then remove the plastic from the top and, holding the dough with your fingertips, peel off the bottom sheet. Lay the tortillas in the skillet, one at a time, and cook about 45 seconds per side, pressing the top with your fingertips to help it puff. Transfer the tortillas to a towel, stacking them as you finish the batch. Serve immediately, or cool, wrap well in plastic, and store in the refrigerator up to a week.

Makes 24 small or 12 large tortillas

flour
tortillas

2¹/₂ cups all-purpose flour

**scant ¹/₂ cup vegetable
    shortening (3¹/₂ ounces)**

1 teaspoon coarse salt

1 cup warm water

Flour tortillas, more popular in the North, are the white bread of the Mexican kitchen. Still, we adore them with richer foods like meat stews and our bean and fish burritos on page 48.

Place the flour, shortening, and salt in the bowl of a heavy-duty mixer. Beat with the paddle until crumbly, 3 to 5 minutes. With the mixer running, gradually add the warm water and continue mixing until the dough is smooth, about 3 minutes.

Divide the dough into 8 pieces. Roll each into a ball and place on a baking sheet or board. Cover with a towel and let rest 15 minutes to 1 hour.

Have ready eight 12-inch squares of parchment paper or waxed paper for stacking. On a lightly floured board, roll out each dough ball to a 10-inch circle, and transfer to a paper square. Stack the squares, wrap, and chill until ready to cook.

To cook, heat a dry griddle or nonstick skillet over medium heat. Carefully peel off the paper and cook the tortillas, one at a time, until puffy and slightly brown, about 45 seconds per side. Set aside to cool slightly on a towel-lined platter. Bring to the table wrapped in the towel, or wrap well in plastic and refrigerate or freeze.

Makes 8 large tortillas

latin soups

Susan is passionate about soups, and most of these rustic dishes reflect the kind of brothy meals in a bowl that she likes to eat and serve at home. ■ A good cook can best be judged by how she cooks the simple things, and soup is a terrific place to begin to learn how to cook rather than simply follow a recipe. The method is easy to learn: *First,* sauté the onions or other aromatic vegetables in fat to develop their flavor. *Next,* season with all of your heart and soul—a soup is no place to be timid. *Third,* add a flavorful broth or stock and *fourth,* learn the cooking times of each ingredient so you'll know that delicate foods such as shrimp and herbs go in at the end, while root vegetables cook for a good long time. The *fifth* step is to stop and think about texture—should this be a luxuriously smooth soup or a rustic chunky broth?—and *finally,* taste and season one last time. Often, we like to finish soups with a dollop of salsa or pesto, or a squeeze of lime to heighten and refresh all the flavors.

gazpacho

1/2 slice bread, crusts removed

4 cups high-quality tomato
   juice, plus more if needed

3 ripe Roma tomatoes, cored,
   seeded, and diced

5 pickling cucumbers (Kirbys),
   peeled, seeded, and diced

4 scallions, sliced

1 red bell pepper, cored,
   seeded, and diced

1 small jícama, peeled
   and diced

1/2 cup extra virgin olive oil

3 jalapeños, stemmed, seeded,
   and diced

2 garlic cloves

1 tablespoon red wine vinegar

2 teaspoons sugar

1 teaspoon coarse salt, or
   more to taste

1/2 teaspoon freshly ground
   black pepper, or more
   to taste

sliced chives, for garnish

This easy red gazpacho takes practically no time to put together and holds well in the refrigerator for a day or so. If it does thicken, add some sparkling water to thin it, and adjust the seasonings.

Soak the bread in cold water 15 to 20 minutes; squeeze out the excess moisture.

Combine the tomato juice, tomatoes, cucumbers, scallions, red pepper, and jícama in a large bowl. Transfer about one quarter of the vegetables to a blender, along with the olive oil, jalapeños, garlic, bread, red wine vinegar, sugar, salt, and pepper. Blend until smooth.

Return the puree to the bowl with the vegetables and mix well. Add more tomato juice to thin if needed, and adjust the seasonings. Chill at least 2 hours.

Serve in chilled soup bowls and garnish with chives.

Serves 4 to 6

hot tip
ON CUCUMBERS
We prefer the small pickling cucumbers called Kirbys for salads because they have fewer seeds and hold less water than regular cucumbers. We chop off the ends before peeling, as this is where bitterness is stored. If using large cucumbers, cut in half lengthwise and scrape out the seeds with a teaspoon.

white grape gazpacho

4 slices stale country bread, crusts removed

1 ¹/₂ cups blanched almonds, coarsely chopped

2 garlic cloves, chopped

¹/₂ cup fruity olive oil

¹/₄ cup sherry vinegar

2 cups white grape juice

2 cups ice water

1 tablespoon coarse salt, or to taste

24 seedless white or Muscat grapes, halved

Cold soups have to hit just the right note to really work. Though this one may sound strange, it is quite common in Spain. It is amazingly refreshing as a summer lunch centerpiece, accompanied by a cheese platter and chunks of good bread. Always serve cold soups very cold for maximum effect.

Soak the bread in cold water 15 to 20 minutes.

Meanwhile combine the almonds and garlic in a blender or a food processor and blend until the almonds are very finely ground, almost to a paste. Reserve in the blender.

Squeeze out the excess water from the bread, add to the almonds, and process until smooth. With the motor running, add the oil in a thin stream, then the vinegar, scraping down the sides often. Add the grape juice and ice water 1 cup at a time, blending after each addition. Season with the salt and process briefly to combine. Chill at least 6 hours before serving.

Serve in chilled soup bowls and garnish with the grapes.

Serves 4

sweet plantain soup with pineapple-orange salsa

Salsa

1/2 cup diced fresh or canned
    pineapple

2 blood oranges or other oranges,
    peel and pith removed, cut into
    slices, seeds removed, and diced

1 tablespoon minced fresh ginger

2 serrano chiles, stemmed,
    seeded, and minced

2 tablespoons freshly squeezed
    lime juice

1 teaspoon coarse salt

1/4 teaspoon freshly ground
    black pepper

1 1/2 tablespoons unsalted butter

2 large ripe plantains, sliced

2 teaspoons dried oregano,
    crumbled

2 leeks, white parts only,
    washed and thinly sliced

2 medium parsnips, peeled
    and chopped

3 cups chicken stock

3 cups milk

juice of 1/2 lemon

1 teaspoon coarse salt

1/2 teaspoon freshly ground
    black pepper

This lovely soup gets its tropical fragrance from the combination of plantains and earthy parsnips. It is surprisingly easy to make for such a glamorous dish.

Combine all of the salsa ingredients in a small bowl and gently toss. Cover and refrigerate up to 4 hours.

Heat the butter in a large heavy skillet over medium heat. Sauté the plantain slices until softened and very lightly browned, about 2 minutes per side. Add the oregano and cook 1 minute. Then add the leeks and parsnips and cook 5 minutes longer. Pour in the chicken stock, cover, and cook, stirring occasionally, until all the vegetables are tender, 10 to 15 minutes.

Transfer to a food processor and puree. Pour into a large saucepan or soup pot. Stir in the milk and bring to a boil over medium-high heat. Reduce to a simmer and cook, covered, stirring occasionally, about 10 minutes.

Season with the lemon juice, salt, and pepper. Serve in shallow soup bowls and garnish each with a spoonful of the salsa.

Serves 6

shrimp, corn, and potato chowder

The Latin tradition of tossing rounds of corn on the cob into soup adds an extra dollop of sweet corn flavor along with visual appeal we find hard to resist. This hearty soup is exceptionally sweet from the combination of shrimp, corn, and milk.

1 tablespoon unsalted butter

1 tablespoon olive oil

2 medium onions, finely diced

1 1/2 teaspoons coarse salt, or more to taste

1/2 teaspoon freshly ground black pepper, or more to taste

2 poblano chiles, roasted, peeled, seeded, and diced

4 garlic cloves, finely chopped

6 Roma tomatoes, cored, peeled, seeded, and chopped

3 cups fish stock or clam juice

1 bay leaf

6 small new potatoes, peeled and halved

3 cups milk

1 ear corn, shucked and cut into 1/2-inch lengths

1 cup fresh corn kernels

1 pound medium shrimp, peeled and deveined

1/2 small bunch cilantro, leaves only

Heat the butter and oil in a large heavy saucepan over medium heat. Sauté the onions with the salt and pepper 4 to 5 minutes, until golden. Stir in the poblanos and garlic and cook 2 minutes more, just until the aroma of the garlic is released.

Add the tomatoes, fish stock, and bay leaf. Turn the heat to high and bring to a boil. Add the potatoes, bring back to a boil, and reduce to a simmer. Cover and cook 15 minutes, or until the potatoes are tender but not falling apart.

Add the milk and corn rounds and simmer 10 minutes longer. Then stir in the corn kernels and shrimp and cook 3 minutes. Adjust the seasonings, garnish with the cilantro, and serve.

Serves 6

roasted garlic vegetable soup

2 tablespoons olive oil

1 large onion, diced

2 large carrots, peeled and
  diced

1 large leek, white and light
  green part only, washed
  and diced

1 rib celery, diced

1 bunch thyme, tied together
  with kitchen twine, plus
  6 small sprigs for garnish

2 bay leaves

1 teaspoon coarse salt, or
  more to taste

$^1/_2$ teaspoon freshly ground
  black pepper, or more
  to taste

2 quarts chicken stock,
  preferably homemade

Roasted Garlic, recipe follows,
  cloves peeled

$^3/_4$ cup heavy cream

6 very thin slices French
  bread, toasted and rubbed
  with a split garlic clove

3 tablespoons grated
  Cotija cheese

This strong, comforting peasant soup relies on great homemade chicken stock for a good solid foundation. It makes an excellent starter for an elegant dinner party of Mediterranean foods such as herbed leg of lamb.

Heat the olive oil in a large heavy saucepan over low heat. Add the onion and cook 5 minutes. Add the carrots, leek, celery, thyme, bay leaves, salt, and pepper. Cook, stirring occasionally, about 20 minutes, until the vegetables are very soft and golden. Pour in the stock, increase the heat to high, and bring to a boil. Reduce to a simmer and cook, uncovered, 10 to 20 minutes.

Transfer 1 cup of the stock to a blender. Add the roasted garlic and puree. Pour the garlic mixture back into the soup pot, along with the cream. Adjust the seasonings and continue cooking over medium heat just to heat through. With a slotted spoon, remove the bay leaves and bunch of thyme.

Sprinkle the toasted garlic bread with the grated cheese. Ladle the soup into bowls and top each with a slice of garlic cheese bread and a sprig of thyme. Serve hot.

Serves 6

roasted garlic

1 large head garlic (whole and unpeeled)

2 tablespoons extra virgin olive oil

$\frac{1}{2}$ teaspoon dried oregano, crumbled

$\frac{1}{2}$ teaspoon coarse salt

$\frac{1}{2}$ teaspoon freshly ground black pepper

Preheat the oven to 350°F.

With a sharp knife, slice about $\frac{1}{2}$ inch off the top of the head of garlic. Stack two 6-inch squares of aluminum foil. Place the garlic in the center and lift the sides to form a cup. Drizzle with the olive oil and sprinkle with the oregano, salt, and pepper. Enclose by twisting the edges of the foil together to seal.

Place on a baking sheet and roast 20 to 25 minutes, until entirely softened. Open the foil and set aside to cool. When cool enough to handle, squeeze to remove the garlic cloves, discarding the skins.

shellfish egg-drop soup

2 cups chunked stale
   country bread

$^1/_4$ cup fruity olive oil

1 teaspoon coarse salt

$^1/_2$ teaspoon freshly ground
   black pepper

2 cups dry white wine

1 dozen small clams, well
   scrubbed

1 pound mussels, well
   scrubbed

5 cups fish stock or clam juice

$^1/_2$ bunch cilantro, leaves only,
   plus cilantro sprigs, for
   garnish

4 garlic cloves

juice of $^1/_2$ lime, or to taste

1 pound large shrimp, shelled,
   deveined, and cut into
   $^1/_2$-inch pieces

2 large eggs, lightly beaten

A hearty shellfish soup such as this açorda from Portugal makes a wonderful summer supper, with just some crusty bread and a green salad. Feel free to substitute chunked fish or whatever shellfish looks best at the market.

Preheat the oven to 350°F.

Toss together the bread cubes, 2 tablespoons of the olive oil, $^1/_2$ teaspoon of the salt, and $^1/_4$ teaspoon of the pepper. Spread the cubes on a baking sheet and toast until golden, 8 to 10 minutes. Set aside.

Combine the wine and clams in a large saucepan or stockpot over medium-high heat. Cover and cook, shaking the pan occasionally, until the clams open, about 10 minutes. With a slotted spoon, transfer the clams to a bowl, discarding any that remain closed. Add the mussels and repeat the procedure. Transfer the mussels to the bowl with the clams and let cool. Set the pan aside.

Remove all the meat from the shells and set aside in a bowl covered with a damp towel. Discard the shells and add the liquor from the bowl to the pan of wine. Strain this liquid through a fine strainer lined with cheesecloth into a large saucepan. Pour in the stock.

In a mini food processor, combine the cilantro, garlic, the remaining 2 tablespoons olive oil, the lime juice, and the remaining $^1/_2$ teaspoon salt and $^1/_4$ teaspoon pepper and process to a paste. Set aside.

Bring the wine and clam juice mixture to a simmer and add the cooked shellfish and the shrimp. Simmer for 3 minutes. Add the bread chunks and stir for 2 minutes over low heat. Add the beaten eggs in a slow, steady stream, stirring briskly to disperse the threads. Spoon the cilantro paste into the bottom of six serving bowls. Ladle in the hot soup and garnish with cilantro sprigs.

Serves 6

hot tip

TO CLARIFY CHICKEN FAT

As restaurant cooks, we've been well trained in the frugalities of running a professional kitchen. As a result, we would never think of wasting the fat that rises to the top of a good chicken stock. We like to skim it off, clarify it, and have it on hand for delicious sautéed chicken dishes and to add an extra dollop of flavor to vegetables and lovely bean soups.

To clarify chicken fat, place the collected fat in a small heavy saucepan. Cook at a low simmer until the water evaporates and the bubbling stops. Let cool, then strain and transfer the clear yellow fat to a storage container. It will keep for many weeks in the refrigerator and almost indefinitely in the freezer.

hot tip

HOW TO SKIM A STOCK

When making soup or stock, simmer, don't boil, the liquid. Rapid boiling pulls all of the impurities out of the bones and other ingredients and then emulsifies them into the soup. Use a ladle to remove the scum containing the impurities that rise to the surface. Position the ladle just barely under the surface and skim off and discard only the top layer. Do not disturb the broth too much.

zarzuela de mariscos

1/2 cup Spanish olive oil

2 medium onions, finely chopped

2 red bell peppers, cored, seeded, and julienned

4 large garlic cloves, minced

2 ounces prosciutto, julienned

3 pounds ripe tomatoes, cored, peeled, seeded, and chopped (or use 2 pounds canned tomatoes, seeded and chopped)

1/2 cup ground blanched almonds

1 teaspoon dried thyme

1/2 teaspoon saffron threads (or a pinch of ground saffron)

2 sprigs fresh rosemary, leaves only, finely chopped

2 teaspoons coarse salt, or more to taste

1/2 teaspoon freshly ground black pepper, or more to taste

1/2 teaspoon red pepper flakes

1 cup dry white wine

3 1/2 cups fish stock or half clam juice and half water

juice of 1/2 lemon

12 clams, well scrubbed

12 mussels, well scrubbed

6 jumbo shrimp in the shell

1 pound scallops

1 pound squid, cleaned and cut into rings

6 lemon wedges, for garnish

wedges of grilled country bread, for serving

A Spanish zarzuela is a big, hearty broth similar to a French bouillabaisse, seasoned with saffron and studded with lots of seafood. Break the bank and purchase real saffron threads rather than the ground powder, which is often adulterated with other less costly spices, like turmeric.

Heat the olive oil in a large pot over medium heat. Sauté the onions until translucent, about 5 minutes. Add the bell peppers and garlic and cook 2 to 3 minutes, or until softened. Stir in the prosciutto and cook 3 minutes longer, stirring occasionally. Add the tomatoes and increase the heat to medium-high. Cook, stirring frequently to prevent scorching, until all the liquid has evaporated. Stir in the ground almonds, thyme, saffron, rosemary, salt, black pepper, red pepper flakes, and wine. Bring to a boil and boil until most of the wine has evaporated.

Pour in the fish stock and lemon juice. Bring to a boil and stir in the clams and mussels. Reduce the heat to medium, cover, and cook 10 minutes. Add the shrimp, scallops, and squid and cook 5 minutes longer. Remove and discard any unopened shellfish. Adjust the seasonings and bring to the table. Serve family style in soup bowls, with the lemon wedges and toasted bread.

Serves 6

mexican chicken rice soup

1 (2 to 2½ pound) chicken, rinsed and patted dry

Coarse salt and freshly ground black pepper

2 quarts chicken stock

1 medium carrot, peeled and chopped

2 leeks, white and tender green parts only, washed and chopped

1 chayote (unpeeled), pitted and chopped

⅔ cup short-grain rice

juice of 1 lime

6 tablespoons finely chopped fresh epazote or mint

For the very best chicken soup, always simmer, never boil the stock; include chicken heads and feet if possible; and cook whole chicken on the bone for maximum flavor. Shred the chicken in large strips for this comforting peasant soup.

Season the chicken all over with salt and pepper and combine with the stock in a large pot. Bring to a boil, reduce to a simmer, and cook, uncovered, 30 minutes. Add the vegetables and rice and cook 20 minutes longer. Remove from the heat and cool the chicken in the stock.

Lift the chicken from the stock and remove and discard the skin and bones. Shred the chicken and return to the pot. Stir in the lime juice and epazote and reheat the soup. Serve hot.

Serves 6

ropa
vieja

½ pound pork loin or pork
butt, sliced into strips

½ pound tri-tip, skirt, or flank
steak, sliced into strips

Coarse salt and freshly ground
black pepper

2 tablespoons vegetable oil

2 small onions, thinly sliced

4 garlic cloves, minced

2 ribs celery, diced

1 medium carrot, peeled
and diced

2 poblano chiles, roasted,
peeled, seeded, and
julienned

1 red bell pepper, roasted,
peeled, seeded, and
julienned

1 quart chicken stock

1 (15-ounce) can black beans,
with their liquid

6 tablespoons red wine
vinegar

½ bunch cilantro, leaves only,
chopped

Flour Tortillas, page 56,
toasted, for serving

Fresh Salsa, page 18, for
garnish

Traditionally, in Cuba, ropa vieja (literally, "old clothes") is a simple stew of leftover scraps of meat and whatever vegetables happen to be in the house. Served with warm tortillas and beer, our version makes a quick, satisfying hot meal for two.

Season the meats all over with salt and pepper. Heat the oil in a large heavy saucepan over medium-high heat. Sauté the pork and beef until browned all over. Remove from the pan.

Add the onions, 1 teaspoon salt, and ½ teaspoon pepper and sauté until the onions are golden. Then add the garlic and cook briefly, just to release its aroma. Stir in the celery, carrot, poblanos, and red pepper and cook 2 minutes longer.

Pour in the chicken stock. Bring to a boil, reduce to a simmer, and cook 10 minutes. Return the meats, with their juices, to the pan, add the beans, vinegar, and cilantro, and bring just to a simmer. Serve with flour tortillas and salsa fresca.

Serves 4

salads

When it comes to salads, our paths diverge. Mary Sue never skips her greens, and Susan prefers heartier starch-based salads, with pasta or rice, or composed vegetable salads. Our tastes do converge, though, on the matter of dressings. We like them strong and assertive, with unusual touches such as avocado, sherry vinegar, or blanched garlic. Strong dressings, like the Avocado Dressing on page 81, can double as dips or quick sauces for grilled fish. ■ Mary Sue, who eats a salad every night with her family for dinner, speeds up prep time by washing and drying her salad greens at the beginning of the week and then wrapping them in paper towels and storing them in airtight plastic bags in the vegetable bin of the refrigerator. When she comes home from work, all she has to do is whip up a salad dressing and pan-toast some croutons or seeds for an instant crunchy dinner salad. ■ If you want to plan a selection of salads for a buffet, once again, think about balance. At the restaurant, when we design a three-salad plate—a popular item in southern California restaurants—we try to have a starch, a legume, and a vegetable salad. Two nice trios would be the Three-Bean Salad, Parsley and Mint Salad, and Mexican Macaroni Salad, or the Quinoa Salad, Carrot and Currant Salad, and Mimosa Salad. Enjoy, and don't forget to eat your greens!

carrot and currant salad

1 tablespoon Dijon mustard

3 tablespoons sherry vinegar

$\frac{1}{2}$ teaspoon coarse salt

$\frac{1}{2}$ teaspoon freshly ground
   black pepper

$\frac{1}{3}$ cup fruity Spanish olive oil

$\frac{1}{3}$ cup amontillado, cream, or
   other full-flavored sherry

$\frac{3}{4}$ cup currants or dark raisins

1 $\frac{1}{2}$ pounds tender young
   carrots (unpeeled), finely
   julienned or grated

Sherry vinegar is one of our latest passions. It is much less expensive than balsamic and delivers a similar tart/sweet punch to salad dressings and marinades. In this updated American classic, sherry and currants add an interesting new twist. Susan can't stop eating it.

In a large serving bowl, whisk together the mustard, vinegar, salt, pepper, and olive oil. Set aside.

Combine the sherry with the currants in a small saucepan and bring to a boil over medium heat. Remove from the heat and set aside to plump and cool about 20 minutes.

To serve, add the carrots and the currants, with all of their soaking liquid, to the bowl with the vinaigrette. Toss to combine and coat evenly, and serve immediately.

Serves 6

watercress and tangerine salad

We have been playing with variations on the citrus-plus-greens theme since first tasting it in Mexico. The combination is always a great refresher to serve with heartier meats and saucy foods.

3 tablespoons white wine
   vinegar

1 tablespoon Dijon mustard

$1/2$ teaspoon coarse salt, or
   to taste

2 teaspoons cracked black
   pepper

$1/4$ teaspoon cayenne pepper

scant $1/2$ cup extra virgin
   olive oil

1 medium red onion, thinly
   sliced crosswise and soaked
   in ice water for up to 2
   hours, to crisp and mellow

2 tangerines, peel and pith
   removed, cut into slices,
   seeds removed, and diced

2 bunches watercress, coarse
   stems removed, washed
   and dried

To make the vinaigrette, whisk together the vinegar, mustard, salt, black pepper, cayenne, and olive oil in a small bowl.

Drain the onion, pat dry with paper towels, and separate into rings.

In a large bowl, combine the tangerines, watercress, and onion and gently toss. Drizzle with just enough vinaigrette to coat lightly, toss again, and serve.

Serves 6

parsley and mint salad with chipotle vinaigrette

6 large garlic cloves, thinly sliced

2 tablespoons freshly squeezed lemon juice

2 tablespoons freshly squeezed orange juice

1 teaspoon coarse salt

$^1/_2$ teaspoon freshly ground black pepper

$^1/_3$ cup olive oil

2-4 Pickled Chipotles, page 15, stemmed, seeded, and minced

2 bunches Italian parsley, leaves and tender stems only

1 bunch mint, leaves only

As inveterate salad eaters, we have fallen in love with the mixed herb salads sold at our local farmers' market. Fresh herbs deliver such a pleasant burst of spicy flavor in a part of the meal that can be dull—now almost all of our homemade salads are a mixture of lettuce and herbs. Basil, tarragon, sorrel, mint, and chives are all great for eating fresh. This particular all-herb salad was designed as a bed for the crab cakes on page 112, but it makes a sophisticated starter all by itself.

Bring a small pan of lightly salted water to a boil. Add the sliced garlic and blanch about 2 minutes. Drain and set aside.

Whisk together the lemon juice, orange juice, salt, pepper, and olive oil in a small bowl. Stir in the minced chiles and garlic.

Place the herbs in a large bowl. Pour on the dressing and toss well to coat evenly.

Serves 6

mimosa
salad

3 tablespoons Dijon mustard

$^1/_2$ teaspoon coarse salt

$^1/_2$ teaspoon freshly ground
   black pepper

3 tablespoons Champagne
   vinegar

2 medium shallots, finely
   chopped

$^1/_2$ cup extra virgin olive oil

2 heads butter lettuce,
   washed, dried, and torn into
   bite-sized pieces

3 hard-boiled large eggs,
   whites and yolks separated
   and pressed through a sieve

What a perfect way to begin a heavier meal—a delicate salad of soft green lettuce leaves sprinkled with sieved egg so that it resembles the mimosa tree in bloom. Hard-boiled eggs can be overcooked, so be careful not to simmer longer than fifteen minutes, then immediately rinse with cold water and chill.

Whisk together the mustard, salt, pepper, vinegar, shallots, and olive oil in a small bowl.

In a large bowl, combine the lettuce with enough dressing to coat generously. Toss well. Place a mound of the salad on each of six plates and garnish generously with the sieved egg white and yolk.

Serves 6

hot tip
WASHING THE GREENS
The best way to clean lettuces and herbs is to fill a big bowl or
sink with cold water. Add the greens, toss well, and let soak five to
ten minutes. Then gently lift out the leaves and shake off excess moisture.
All the sand and grit will remain at the bottom of the bowl or sink. We like to
spin leaves dry, wrap them in paper towels, and then store in Ziploc
bags in the vegetable bin of the refrigerator, where they are
ready when we are. Wash leeks this way too—as they
can be riddled with sand.

wilted spinach salad with pickled shallots

3 tablespoons sherry vinegar

1 tablespoon Dijon mustard

1 teaspoon coarse salt

$\frac{1}{2}$ teaspoon freshly ground
   black pepper

$\frac{1}{2}$ cup extra virgin olive oil

2 small bunches spinach,
   stems removed, washed,
   and dried

10 Pickled Shallots, recipe
   follows, sliced into rings

$\frac{1}{2}$ cup pepitas, toasted
   (see Note)

$\frac{1}{2}$ cup crumbled feta or añejo
   cheese (optional)

Scott Linquist, chef at Border Grill, taught us this terrific technique for wilting spinach leaves right in the bowl. It immediately opens the leaves' pores so they absorb the dressing quickly—necessitating only a small amount of dressing for lots of flavor.

In a small bowl, whisk together the vinegar, mustard, salt, pepper, and olive oil.

Just before serving, assemble all of the ingredients for the salad on the counter. Turn on a stovetop burner to medium-high. Set a large stainless steel bowl over the burner and heat until very hot. Using an oven mitt or pot holder to protect your hands, pour the vinaigrette into the bowl and swirl for a minute or two, until the vinaigrette is hot. Quickly throw in the spinach and shallots and toss the salad with tongs to coat evenly. When the spinach begins to wilt, remove from the heat and transfer to serving plates. Sprinkle with the toasted pepitas and the cheese if desired. Serve immediately.

Serves 4 to 6

Note: To toast pepitas, heat a dry skillet over medium heat and add the seeds. Toast, shaking the pan frequently, until lightly browned. Remove from the heat and add a dash of soy sauce, swirling the pan to coat the pepitas evenly. Add to salads while still warm.

pickled
shallots

1 cup red wine vinegar

1 cup dry red wine

$^1/_2$ cup packed brown sugar

2 tablespoons black
   peppercorns

1 tablespoon mustard seeds

2 teaspoons red pepper flakes

2 tablespoons coarse salt

20 medium shallots, peeled

Combine the vinegar, wine, brown sugar, peppercorns, mustard seeds, chile flakes, and salt in a medium saucepan. Stir over low heat until the sugar has dissolved. Add the shallots and bring to a boil. Reduce to a simmer and cook 5 minutes. Set aside to cool completely in the liquid.

Transfer the shallots and all their liquid to a jar or plastic container. Cover tightly and store in the refrigerator up to 2 weeks.

Makes about 2 cups

ensalada de green goddess

1 pound zucchini

3 ounces panela cheese, diced

1 bunch scallions, sliced

2 poblano chiles, roasted,
   seeded, peeled, and
   julienned

coarse salt and freshly ground
   black pepper to taste

1/2 cup Spanish pimiento-
   stuffed green olives, sliced

Avocado Dressing,
   recipe follows

Steaming zucchini whole, as we saw cooks do in Greece, locks in more vegetable flavor while keeping the texture firm. Prepare the luscious, creamy dressing a day in advance to allow the flavors to ripen in the refrigerator.

Steam the whole zucchini over simmering water until softened through but not mushy, 6 to 8 minutes. Cut into thick slices.

Combine all of the ingredients just to coat the vegetables except the dressing in a bowl and toss. Add enough dressing and gently toss. Chill at least 30 minutes before serving.

Serves 4 to 6

avocado dressing

1 avocado, halved, seeded, and peeled

juice of 2 lemons

$^1/_3$ cup mayonnaise

1 serrano chile, stemmed and seeded

$^1/_2$ small onion, minced

1 tablespoon honey

1 tablespoon Worcestershire sauce

1 garlic clove, minced

1 teaspoon coarse salt

$^1/_4$ teaspoon cayenne pepper

Mash the avocado with the lemon juice in a bowl. Transfer to a blender, add the remaining ingredients, and puree until smooth. Pour the dressing into a container, cover, and allow to mellow in the refrigerator up to 2 days.

Makes 1 cup

hot tip

HOW TO TOSS A SALAD

A well-dressed salad is a good indication of a careful cook. Begin with cold, crisp, dry greens and place them in a bowl approximately twice as large as the quantity of greens. Whisk the dressing in another bowl and slowly add, tossing with your hands and tasting as you go so you add just the right amount of dressing. Each leaf should be coated, without leaving a pool of dressing on the bottom of the bowl. You can always add more, so add sparingly.
For quick, simple salads at home, we like to season the leaves first with salt and pepper and then drizzle in vinegar or citrus juice and oil sparingly, tossing and tasting as we go, and stopping at just the right moment.

quinoa salad

3/4 pound quinoa, preferably
   organic

1/4 cup freshly squeezed
   lime juice

1 teaspoon coarse salt, or
   more to taste

1/2 teaspoon freshly ground
   black pepper, or more
   to taste

2 jalapeño chiles, stemmed,
   seeded if desired, and
   minced

1/2 cup olive oil

1 large cucumber, peeled,
   seeded, and diced

1 medium tomato, cored,
   seeded, and diced

6 scallions, white parts only,
   thinly sliced

1 bunch Italian parsley, leaves
   only, chopped

1 bunch mint, leaves only,
   chopped

Take a break from tabbouleh with this cool grain salad enhanced with chiles and lime. Remember to find organic quinoa for its less bitter flavor.

Wash the quinoa in a bowl of cold water, rubbing it between your hands and changing the water until the water runs clear.

In a large saucepan, combine the quinoa with about 6 cups of cold water. Bring to a boil, stirring occasionally. Reduce to a simmer and cook 10 to 15 minutes, until just cooked (quinoa is done when all the grains are translucent). Drain well in a fine sieve. Fluff with a fork and let cool or spread on a towel or cookie sheet to cool quickly.

In a small bowl, whisk together the lime juice, salt, pepper, jalapeños and olive oil.

In a large bowl, combine the cooled quinoa with the cucumber, tomato, scallions, parsley, and mint. Toss to mix, then add the lime juice dressing and toss to coat evenly. Adjust the seasonings. Arrange the radicchio leaves on serving plates, mound the salad into the leaves, and garnish with the capers, eggs, feta, and olives.

Serves 6

Garnishes

1 small head radicchio, leaves
   separated

3 tablespoons capers, rinsed

hard-boiled quail eggs,
   halved, or quartered
   hard-boiled eggs

$\frac{1}{4}$ pound feta cheese, crumbled

oil- or brine-cured black olives,
   pitted

hot tip

FRESHLY GROUND BLACK PEPPER

As soon as you start taking yourself seriously as a cook, you owe it to yourself to invest in a good peppermill and switch from ground pepper to peppercorns. The difference will amaze you. We nearly always use black pepper and we grind as we go. Freshly ground pepper adds a wonderfully bright, aromatic perfume that is unlike any other.

High-quality pepper mills have metal grinding teeth on the bottom and an adjustable knob at the top. The looser the knob, the larger the grind. We like large mills that have a handle rather than a movable top for grinding, since it is less tiresome for the wrist. Mary Sue, a devoted pepper head, carries a miniature mill in her purse for dining out.

three-bean salad with bacon dressing

If you are into smoked foods, try smoking the dried beans for an extra dash of flavor. As for beans and bacon, need we say more?

^{1}/3 cup black beans, rinsed, picked over, and soaked overnight

^{1}/3 cup red kidney beans, rinsed, picked over, and soaked overnight

1 ^{1}/2 cups green beans, trimmed and cut on the diagonal into 1-inch lengths

2 slices bacon, thinly sliced

2 tablespoons vegetable oil

3 tablespoons white wine vinegar

1 tablespoon honey

1 tablespoon Dijon mustard

^{1}/2 teaspoon coarse salt, or to taste

^{1}/2 teaspoon freshly ground black pepper

4 jalapeño chiles, stemmed, seeded if desired, and minced

lemon wedges, for garnish

Drain the dried beans, keeping them separate. In each of two medium saucepans, bring 2^1/2 cups of water to a boil. Add the black beans to one pan and the red beans to the other. Cover, reduce to a simmer, and cook until the beans are tender but not falling apart, about 1 hour; add more water if necessary to keep the beans covered. Drain the beans, cover with a damp towel, and set aside to cool.

Bring a medium saucepan of salted water to a boil. Cook the green beans until just tender, 3 to 4 minutes. Drain and spread on paper towels to cool. Then transfer to a plate and chill.

Fry the bacon in a medium skillet until crisp, and drain on paper towels. Transfer 1 tablespoon of the bacon fat to a small bowl and add the oil, vinegar, honey, mustard, salt, pepper, and jalapeños. Whisk until smooth.

Combine all of the beans in a large serving bowl. Pour on the dressing and gently toss to coat evenly. Scatter bacon pieces over the top and serve with lemon wedges.

Serves 4 to 6

mexican macaroni salad

1/2 cup olive oil

1/4 cup red wine vinegar

3 garlic cloves, minced

coarse salt and freshly ground
    black pepper to taste

1 pound penne pasta, cooked,
    drained, and tossed with
    olive oil just to coat

1 cup julienned panela cheese

1 small red onion, chopped

3 pickling cucumbers (Kirbys),
    peeled and chopped

3 Roma tomatoes, cored,
    seeded, and chopped

1/3 cup capers, drained

1 bunch oregano, leaves only,
    chopped

2 serrano chiles, stemmed,
    seeded, and minced

Pasta salads are good solid crowd pleasers for picnics and buffets. This one combines a Mediterranean-style vegetable salad with our favorite mild white Mexican cheese and some chiles to heat things up.

To make the dressing, place the oil, vinegar, garlic, and salt and pepper in a jar. Cover and shake to mix well.

Combine the pasta, cheese, onion, cucumbers, tomatoes, capers, oregano, and serranos in a large bowl. Add the dressing and toss until well coated. Adjust the seasonings and chill before serving.

Serves 6 to 8

cracked crab with three dressings

3 whole Dungeness crabs or
1 1/2 pounds crabmeat,
picked over for shells
and cartilage

Salsa Verde, recipe follows

Pine Nut Salsa, recipe follows

Pimiento Salsa, recipe follows

Fresh boiled crab is a great treat for informal gatherings. We like to line the table with newspaper and let people pick their own. Here we serve it with a variety of sauces: a rich, nutty pumpkin seed sauce, an egg and pine nut blend, and a wonderful roasted red pepper sauce from northern Spain.

To cook the crabs, if using fresh ones, in a very large stockpot, bring about 6 quarts of water to a boil. Plunge the crabs headfirst into the water and cook 12 minutes once the water returns to a boil. Remove the crabs with tongs and let cool.

Remove the triangular belly flap from female crabs and discard. Turn the crabs over and, starting from the rear, pull off the top shell from each and discard. Pull off and discard the spongy fingers from the body and the tiny paddles from the front. Scoop out the orange crab butter and reserve for another use if desired.

Cut the bodies into quarters and twist off the claws and legs and crack, using a heavy nutcracker or a small hammer. Serve on a large platter or newspaper-lined table with the following dipping sauces and lots of lemon wedges.

Serves 6 to 8

salsa verde

3 garlic cloves, peeled

1 to 2 serrano chiles, stemmed
   and seeded if desired

¹/₄ cup raw pumpkin seeds

2 poblano chiles, roasted,
   peeled, and seeded

³/₄ cup chopped fresh Italian
   parsley

¹/₂ bunch cilantro, leaves only,
   chopped

¹/₄ cup olive oil

juice of 1 lime

about ³/₄ cup water

coarse salt and freshly ground
   black pepper

In a dry heavy skillet, toast the garlic and serranos over medium heat until slightly charred. Remove. Add the pumpkin seeds to the skillet and toast until browned. Transfer the garlic, serranos, and seeds to a blender, along with the poblanos, herbs, oil, and lime juice. Blend, adding water as necessary, until a smooth thick dipping paste, like pesto, is formed. Season with salt and pepper and blend to combine.

Makes about 1¹/₂ cups

pine nut
salsa

³/₄ cup pine nuts

3 hard-boiled large egg yolks

2 tablespoons capers

2 tablespoons brine from
   the capers

1 cup half-and-half

coarse salt and freshly ground
   black pepper

Combine the pine nuts, egg yolks, capers and juice, and the half-and-half in a blender and puree until smooth. Season with salt and pepper and blend to combine.

Makes about 1¹/₂ cups

hot tip

HOW TO SHARPEN A VEGETABLE PEELER

The humble vegetable peeler may be the oldest tool in your kitchen, and chances are it has never been sharpened—but it can be. Here is how: Scrape the back side, between the blades, with the back of the tip of a paring knife to remove burrs. Then scrape the front side with the back of the knife. For the most efficient way to peel, always point the item being peeled downward, stabilizing it on a board (not holding it in the air), and peel down and away from yourself.

pimiento
salsa

2 red bell peppers, roasted, peeled, seeded, and cut into chunks

4 hard-boiled large egg yolks

1 cup half-and-half

2 tablespoons olive oil

1 tablespoon anchovy paste

1 teaspoon paprika

$1/2$ teaspoon coarse salt

$1/4$ teaspoon freshly ground black pepper

3 tablespoons freshly squeezed lemon juice

dash of Tabasco

20 Spanish pimiento-stuffed green olives, finely chopped

In a blender, combine the red peppers, egg yolks, half-and-half, oil, anchovy paste, paprika, salt, and pepper. Blend until smooth. Pour into a bowl and stir in the lemon juice, Tabasco, and olives.

Makes about 2 cups

smoked swordfish salad mazatlán

1 (³/₄-pound) swordfish steak

coarse salt and freshly ground
    black pepper

¹/₂ cup cider vinegar

3 large garlic cloves, minced

1 teaspoon sugar

²/₃ cup olive oil

3 scallions, white and light
    green parts only, finely
    chopped

¹/₂ avocado, seeded, peeled,
    and diced

1 small white onion, very
    thinly sliced crosswise and
    soaked in ice water for up
    to 2 hours, to crisp and
    mellow

1 bunch spinach, stems
    removed, washed, dried, and
    torn into bite-sized pieces

1 head butter lettuce, washed,
    dried, and torn into bite-
    sized pieces

1 pint cherry tomatoes, halved

Cider vinegar is a neglected American staple that has been pushed aside in favor of more costly Italian vinegars. We recommend shopping at health food markets for deliciously mild unfiltered organic apple cider vinegars.

Prepare a smoker for hot smoking by soaking and then igniting three large hardwood chunks. Regulate the temperature to remain between 170° and 250°F.

Season the swordfish on both sides with salt and pepper. Smoke the fish 30 to 45 minutes, or until it is flaky and cooked through but still moist. Shred the fish and refrigerate.

Whisk together the vinegar, garlic, 1 teaspoon salt, 1½ teaspoons pepper, the sugar, and olive oil in a small bowl. Stir in the scallions and diced avocado, and adjust the seasonings.

To serve, drain the onion slices, pat dry, and separate into rings. Place the spinach, lettuce, and tomatoes in a large bowl and gently toss to coat. Mound the salad on each of six serving plates and scatter the shredded swordfish over the salads. Garnish each with a few onion rings and serve.

Serves 6

hot tip

TO IMPROVISE A SMOKER

The many kettle-style home smokers on the market must be used outdoors. Indoors, we like to improvise with a wok. Soak hardwood chips at least three hours. Line the wok with aluminum foil and place the soaked wood chips in the bottom. Set a round metal wok rack above the wood. Place the wok over medium heat, partially covered, until the wood begins to smoke. Arrange the food on a plate on the rack and partially cover. Keep the heat just high enough so the chips smolder.

main courses

The common theme in all of our centerpiece dishes is their robust flavor and rustic personality. Many are roasts or stews that just naturally develop deep, full flavors by slow cooking. Even those that are sautés are kept simple by making a quick sauce in the same pan. ■ We are big believers in staying close to the elementary nature of things by cooking poultry, fish, and meats whole, on the bone, for maximum flavor and dining pleasure. Chewing on bones is every eater's inalienable right, and if you've given it up in favor of more refined eating, all the more reason now to cook up some messy ribs or a whole chicken and gnaw on some bones. ■ We are proudest, however, of our full-bodied vegetarian entrées. It takes a bit more work to build a great vegetable main course, but it is always a welcome break for those who crave more variety in their diet, as we do. These are all special and strong enough to take center stage.

from the coop

arroz con pollo

1 (2½- to 3-pound) chicken, rinsed, patted dry, and cut into 6 or 8 serving pieces

coarse salt and freshly ground black pepper

1 tablespoon vegetable oil

3 tablespoons unsalted butter

4 ounces fine noodles, such as fideo or capellini, broken into 1-inch lengths

1 large onion, finely chopped

1 large garlic clove, minced

1 tablespoon paprika

3 Roma tomatoes, cored and coarsely chopped

1½ cups short-grain rice

1 cup fresh or frozen baby peas

pinch of saffron threads, crushed, or ⅛ teaspoon ground saffron

3 cups boiling water

½ bunch Italian parsley, leaves only, roughly chopped

Toasted fideo or other thin pasta gives a new twist to one of the best-known comfort foods of the Spanish-American kitchen. It adds the nutty, toasted wheat flavor we adore.

Season the chicken pieces generously with salt and pepper.

Heat the oil in a large heavy ovenproof casserole over medium-high heat. Add the chicken and cook until browned all over. Transfer to a platter and set aside.

Drain the fat from the pan and add the butter. Place over medium heat and toss in the noodles. Cook, stirring constantly, until well browned, 6 to 8 minutes. Reduce the heat to low and add the onion. Cook, stirring occasionally, 4 to 5 minutes, until softened. Add the garlic and cook 1 to 2 minutes, until it releases its aroma. Add the paprika and tomatoes and cook, stirring frequently, about 5 minutes, or until most of the liquid has evaporated. Return chicken to casserole.

Stir in the rice, peas, saffron, boiling water, and 1 teaspoon salt. Bring to a boil over high heat. Reduce to a simmer and cook, covered, 25 to 35 minutes, until the chicken is cooked through and the rice has absorbed all the liquid. Stir in the parsley, cover, and let stand 5 minutes before serving.

Serves 4 to 6

country chicken stew

1 (2½-pound) chicken, rinsed,
   patted dry, and cut into
   8 serving pieces

coarse salt and freshly ground
   black pepper

2 tablespoons olive oil

30 cipollini or pearl onions,
   peeled

¾ pound carrots, peeled and
   sliced into ½-inch rounds

8 small Red or White Rose
   potatoes

1 bay leaf

1 cup dry white wine

4 cups chicken stock,
   preferably homemade

Picada

2½ ounces slivered almonds,
   toasted

3 large garlic cloves, peeled

½ teaspoon loosely packed
   saffron threads

3 hard-boiled large egg yolks

3 hard-boiled large egg whites,
   finely chopped

Picada—almonds, garlic, and saffron, ground to a paste and thickened with hard-boiled egg yolks—is a typical Catalan way to finish a stew. Serve this rustic chicken dish with a Rioja wine and plenty of good, crusty bread.

Season the chicken generously with salt and pepper. Heat the olive oil in a large heavy skillet over medium-high heat. Brown the chicken evenly on all sides, then transfer to a flameproof casserole. Add the onions and carrots to the skillet and cook, stirring occasionally, until golden, about 10 minutes. Transfer to the casserole with the chicken. Place the potatoes around the edges and season with 2 teaspoons salt and 1 teaspoon pepper. Add bay leaf.

Pour off most of the fat from the skillet and return to high heat. Pour in the white wine and cook, stirring and scraping the bottom of the pan to release all the browned bits, about 3 minutes. Pour over the chicken and add the stock.

Place the casserole over medium heat and bring to a boil. Reduce to a simmer and cook, covered, 25 to 30 minutes, until the chicken thighs are cooked through. (Check the pan occasionally to make sure the liquid is at a slow simmer.)

To make the picada, combine the almonds and garlic in a food processor and process to a fine paste. Add the saffron and hard-boiled egg yolks and process again, adding enough liquid from the casserole to make a smooth paste. Set aside.

With a slotted spoon, transfer the chicken and vegetables to a serving tureen, and discard the bay leaf.

Return the casserole to medium-high heat and whisk the picada into the cooking liquid. Pour over the chicken and vegetables, sprinkle with the egg whites, and serve.

Serves 4

cinnamon chicken

1 1/2 cups dry sherry

1/2 cup honey

1/4 cup freshly squeezed
   lemon juice

4 garlic cloves, minced

1 tablespoon ground cinnamon

1 teaspoon coarse salt

1/2 teaspoon freshly ground
   black pepper

1 (2 1/2- to 3-pound) frying
   chicken, rinsed, patted dry,
   and cut into 8 serving
   pieces

2 tablespoons vegetable oil

This exceptionally easy chicken bakes to a golden-brown glaze—the meat oozing with surprising flavors from the marinade. It would be great with simple accompaniments like mashed potatoes or grilled corn on the cob sprinkled with cayenne and lime.

In a large bowl, mix the dry sherry, honey, lemon juice, garlic, cinnamon, salt, and pepper. Add the chicken and toss to coat evenly. Cover and marinate in the refrigerator at least 8 hours, or overnight.

Preheat the oven to 350°F.

Remove the chicken from the marinade, shaking off the excess, and set aside on a plate. Pour the marinade into a small saucepan and bring to a boil. Boil until it is reduced to about 1 cup and beginning to thicken, 5 to 10 minutes. Set aside.

Heat the oil in an ovenproof skillet over medium-high heat. Sear the chicken until golden on all sides. Pour the reduced marinade over the chicken and place in the oven. Bake about 20 minutes, until cooked through. Serve.

Serves 4

hot tip

TIME TO MARINATE

Now that mass-produced meats
like chicken and pork have lost much of
their flavor, we depend on stronger marinades to
put some oomph back into them. A flavorful marinade can
sometimes even take the place of a sauce. As a general rule,
marinades need to be strong to really make a difference. The
shorter the marinating time, the stronger a mixture you need for
the flavors to sink in. For really short times, we sometimes compen-
sate by brushing the meat with the marinade as it cooks. Marinades
will be more effective if they are at the same temperature as the
ingredient being marinated. So, for example, warm beans or lentils
for a salad will absorb a warm marinade better than a cold one.

hot tip

COOL AND DARK IS ESSENTIAL

A cool dark storage area in your kitchen is essential for properly storing most fruits, garlic, onions, potatoes, yams, and eggplant. Be sure to keep potatoes out of sunlight, since that is what promotes that green tinge under the skin which must be removed before eating.

roasted chicken with a papaya glaze

1 (3-pound) chicken

coarse salt and freshly ground
black pepper

1 orange, quartered

1/2 onion, chunked

4 garlic cloves, crushed

1 cup orange juice

1/4 cup olive oil

1/4 cup packed light brown
sugar

2 shallots, halved

2 bay leaves

Papaya Glaze

2 tablespoons Dijon mustard

2 garlic cloves, sliced

1 ripe papaya, halved, peeled,
and seeded, one half diced,
for garnish

1 tablespoon chopped fresh
thyme

1/2 teaspoon coarse salt

1/4 teaspoon freshly ground
black pepper

1 tablespoon cold unsalted
butter

Roasting the chicken breast side down first makes the juices run into the breast, keeping it extra-moist. The bird also gets an extra dollop of moistness and flavor from papaya, which contains an enzyme called papain that acts as a natural meat tenderizer.

Rinse the chicken and pat dry with paper towels. Rub the cavity with salt and pepper. Stuff with the orange, onion, and garlic. Rub the outside with 1 teaspoon salt and 1/2 teaspoon pepper and place in a baking dish just large enough to hold it.

In a blender or a food processor, combine the orange juice, olive oil, brown sugar, and shallots. Process until the shallots are finely minced. Pour over the chicken, crumble the bay leaves over the top, and cover tightly with plastic wrap. Marinate in the refrigerator at least 3 hours, preferably overnight, spooning the marinade over the chicken occasionally.

Preheat the oven to 375°F.

Transfer the chicken to a rack in a roasting pan, breast side down, reserving marinade. Roast the chicken 20 minutes. Prepare the papaya glaze. Pour the marinade into a food processor and add the mustard, garlic, the papaya half, the thyme, salt, and pepper. Process until smooth. Divide the glaze in half. Use half to baste the chicken; reserve the other half for the sauce.

Turn the chicken breast side up and baste with the glaze. Roast 50 to 60 minutes longer, basting every 20 minutes, until golden brown. Transfer to a serving platter, cover with foil, and keep warm at the back of the stove.

To make the sauce, drain the fat from the pan. Add the reserved papaya mixture and place over medium heat. Bring to a simmer, scraping the pan. Whisk in the butter and diced papaya. Transfer to a sauceboat and pass at the table.

Serves 4

red roasted chicken

1 (3-pound) chicken

3 garlic cloves, finely chopped

2 tablespoons paprika

coarse salt and freshly ground
black pepper

¼ cup red wine vinegar

⅓ cup Spanish olive oil

3 tablespoons unsalted butter

2 medium onions, finely
chopped

6 Roma tomatoes, cored,
seeded, and chopped
(or use canned)

½ cup water

½ bunch Italian parsley,
leaves only, roughly
chopped, for garnish

Who doesn't need just one more basic but delicious roasted chicken recipe for Sunday night supper?

Rinse the chicken, remove any excess fat, and pat dry with paper towels. In a small bowl, mix together the garlic, paprika, 2 teaspoons salt, 2 teaspoons pepper, and the vinegar. Rub the vinegar mixture all over the chicken, including the cavity. Cover with plastic wrap and marinate at room temperature 1 hour.

Preheat the oven to 350°F.

Heat a large cast-iron skillet over medium-high heat and add the olive oil. Shake the chicken to drain the excess vinegar. Using kitchen tongs and a large wooden spoon to steady the bird, brown it on all sides in the hot oil. Transfer to a plate and set aside.

Melt the butter in the skillet over medium-high heat. Sauté the onions, with 1 teaspoon salt and ½ teaspoon pepper, 3 to 5 minutes. Add the tomatoes and cook 2 to 3 minutes. Add the water and set the chicken on top of the vegetables. Roast 1 hour, until the leg moves easily when twisted. Transfer the chicken to a serving platter and cover loosely with aluminum foil.

Tip the casserole to one side and spoon off the excess fat. Carve the chicken into serving pieces, and arrange on a platter with the vegetables and juices from the pan. Sprinkle with the parsley and serve.

Serves 4 to 6

hot tip

ROASTING TIPS

· We like to sear meats to be roasted by placing them in a very hot oven—about 450°F—for the first ten to fifteen minutes to caramelize the outside and seal in juices. We prefer high-temperature roasting and shorter cooking times.

· After you roast meats and poultry, it is important not to carve them immediately but to let them rest five to ten minutes. Meat continues to cook outside the oven and as it rests, the flesh relaxes and the juices are absorbed more evenly.

habanero-glazed hens with spicy corn bread stuffing

Stuffing

6 slices bacon, chopped

1 medium onion, chopped

2 ribs celery, chopped

4 jalapeño chiles, stemmed, seeded, and minced

$^3/_4$ cup chicken stock

1 teaspoon coarse salt

$^1/_2$ bunch Italian parsley, leaves only, chopped

$3^1/_2$ cups cubed corn bread, toasted

4 game hens, rinsed and patted dry

coarse salt and freshly ground black pepper

Glaze

1 tablespoon vegetable oil

3 shallots, finely diced

$^1/_2$ cup brandy

$^1/_2$ cup orange juice

$^1/_2$ teaspoon habanero chile powder

Any notions of game hens as nondescript little birds are bound to disappear with one taste of this intensely spicy, sweet orange glaze. Buy habanero chile powder, made from the hottest little chiles of all, in specialty shops or from mail-order sources. If you have whole dried habaneros, grind them in a spice grinder or crush very fine with a knife, first removing the stems and seeds.

Preheat the oven to 375°F.

To make the stuffing, fry the bacon until crisp in a medium cast-iron skillet over medium heat. With a slotted spoon, transfer the bacon to paper towels to drain. Pour off all but 2 tablespoons of the fat from the pan and reserve it.

Return the pan to medium heat and sauté the onion 3 to 5 minutes until translucent. Add the celery and jalapeños and sauté 2 to 3 minutes. Add the stock, the crisp bacon, and the parsley, stir to combine, and remove from the heat.

Place the corn bread in a large bowl. Pour the chicken stock mixture over the bread and toss well. Let cool slightly.

Season the hens inside and out with salt and pepper and fill the cavities loosely with the corn bread stuffing. Truss the hens.

Heat the reserved bacon fat in a large cast-iron skillet over high heat. Sauté the hens until brown on all sides, turning often. Transfer to a roasting pan, place in the oven, and roast 20 minutes.

Make the glaze. Heat the oil in the same skillet and sauté the shallots until golden. Add the brandy, bring to a simmer, and reduce by half. Stir in the orange juice and habanero powder and simmer until slightly thickened. Brush the hens with glaze and roast about 10 minutes longer, brushing occasionally with glaze, until the juices run clear. Transfer the hens to serving plates and serve hot.

Serves 6

hot tip

CHOPPING FRESH HERBS

It is always best to handle fresh herbs gently. Chop by loosely rolling herbs into a ball and slicing first in one direction, then in the other. If you roll back and forth with the knife and crush herbs too much, the leaves will bruise and the valuable oils and delicate flavor will be left on the board. Chop herbs right before you need them and add at the end of cooking time.

chiles relleno de picadillo

Picadillo

2 tablespoons vegetable oil

1 medium onion, diced

1 teaspoon coarse salt

$^1/_2$ teaspoon freshly ground
   black pepper

3 garlic cloves, minced

1 $^1/_2$ pounds ground turkey,
   preferably dark meat

1 teaspoon ground cinnamon

$^1/_4$ teaspoon ground cloves

4 canned Italian plum
   tomatoes, drained and
   chopped

$^1/_3$ cup golden raisins

1 $^1/_2$ tablespoons cider vinegar

$^1/_2$ cup toasted slivered
   almonds

12 large poblano chiles,
   roasted and carefully
   peeled, without tearing

6 large eggs, separated

$^1/_3$ cup plus 1 $^1/_2$ tablespoons
   all-purpose flour

$^3/_4$ teaspoon coarse salt

vegetable oil for frying

Red Salsa, page 19, warmed

Roasted chiles stuffed with sweet-and-spicy meat filling are a traditional Mexican-American border dish. Poblanos are a great chile for stuffing since they are wide at the top and have excellent flavor.

To make the picadillo, heat the oil in a large heavy skillet over medium heat. Sauté the onions with the salt and pepper about 5 minutes, until soft. Add the garlic and cook 2 minutes more. Add the turkey, breaking it up with a wooden spoon and spreading it evenly in the pan. Sauté, stirring frequently and separating any clumps, until thoroughly browned. Add the cinnamon, cloves, tomatoes, raisins, and vinegar. Cook over low heat, stirring occasionally, until the pan is nearly dry, 20 to 25 minutes. Stir in the toasted almonds and set aside to cool.

Make a slit in the side of each roasted chile and carefully scrape out the seeds with your fingers. Loosely stuff the chiles with the picadillo and seal the edges with toothpicks.

In a large bowl, beat the egg whites with the salt to soft peaks. Gently beat in the egg yolks, one at a time, and then gently beat in 1 $^1/_2$ tablespoons of the flour. Stop beating as soon as the flour disappears.

Place the remaining $^1/_3$ cup flour on a plate. Roll the chiles in the flour, gently patting off the excess.

Preheat the oven to 200°F.

Heat about $^3/_4$ inch of vegetable oil in a large heavy skillet over medium-low heat to 375°F. Pick up a chile by its stem and dip into the egg mixture, shaking off the excess. Carefully place in the hot oil, and repeat until the pan is full (but do not crowd). Fry until the chiles are brown on one side and gently turn to brown the other side. With a slotted spoon, transfer to paper towels to drain. Keep warm on a baking sheet in the oven while you dip and fry the remaining chiles.

To serve, ladle about ½ cup of the warmed sauce onto each serving plate. Top each with 2 chiles and serve immediately.

Serves 6

hot tip

HOW TO ROAST FRESH CHILES

Fresh chiles and bell peppers can be roasted directly over a gas or electric burner or on a tray under the broiler. Keep turning so the skin is evenly charred, without burning and drying out the flesh. Transfer the charred peppers to a plastic or paper bag, tie the top closed, and let steam until cool to the touch, about fifteen minutes. (If you are rushed, use a plastic bag and place it in a bowl of ice water to speed things up.) The best way to peel is just to pull off the charred skin and then, if necessary, dip the peppers briefly in water to remove any blackened bits. Do not peel peppers under running water, since that will wash away flavorful juices. Once the peppers are peeled, cut away or pull out stems, seeds, and veins.

turkey braised in black mole

16 medium dried mulato chiles, wiped clean

5 medium dried ancho chiles, wiped clean

6 dried pasilla chiles, wiped clean

3/4 cup vegetable oil, or more if necessary

1/2 pound tomatoes, roasted, (see page 7)

2 ounces semisweet chocolate, broken into chunks

1 teaspoon black peppercorns

3 whole cloves or 1/8 teaspoon ground cloves

3 allspice berries or 1/8 teaspoon ground allspice

1 (2-inch) cinnamon stick or 1 teaspoon ground cinnamon

1/4 cup sesame seeds, plus additional for garnish

1/2 teaspoon coriander seeds or 1/4 teaspoon ground coriander

1/3 cup unblanched almonds

1/3 cup dark raisins

1 small onion, cut into thick slices

4 small garlic cloves, peeled

The key to preparing any long, complex recipe is to read it through and take the time to organize all of the ingredients beforehand. What better bird than turkey, a native of Mexico, to complement that ultimate hybrid of the American Indian and Spanish kitchens, mole? Take your time and do it right, and we promise you won't be disappointed. This recipe doubles nicely for feeding a holiday crowd.

Slit the dried chiles lengthwise and remove and discard the stems, seeds, and veins. Tear into flat pieces. Heat 1/4 cup of the oil in a large heavy skillet over medium heat. Toast the chiles 1 to 2 minutes per side, until browned; do not burn. With a slotted spoon, transfer the chiles to a bowl. Pour in enough warm water to cover and soak, covered, 3-4 hours or overnight.

To make the sauce, combine the roasted tomatoes and chocolate in a large bowl. Break up the tomatoes with a spoon, and set aside.

If using whole spices, combine the peppercorns, cloves, allspice, and cinnamon in a spice grinder, or use a mortar and pestle, and finely grind the spices. Add the freshly or ready-ground spices to the tomato mixture.

Place the sesame seeds in a large dry skillet over low heat and toast briefly, until golden. Add the seeds to the tomato mixture and repeat the toasting process with the coriander seeds; or add the ground coriander to the tomatoes.

In the same skillet, heat 1/4 cup of the oil over medium heat. Add the almonds and sauté, stirring occasionally, until well browned. With a slotted spoon, transfer to the tomato mixture. Repeat this procedure, separately, with the raisins, the onion and garlic, the tortillas, and bread. Be sure to drain each ingredient of excess fat before transferring to the tomatoes, and break the tortillas and bread into large pieces. Add a bit

2 Corn Tortillas, page 55,
    stale or dried in the oven

2 thick slices French bread,
    stale or dried in the oven

7 to 8 cups turkey or
    chicken stock

1 canned chipotle chile,
    seeded (optional)

2 turkey legs with thighs, cut
    though the joints

coarse salt and freshly ground
    black pepper

$1/4$ cup packed brown sugar
    or pilloncillo

more oil to the pan if necessary. Stir the tomato mixture well.

In a blender or food processor, combine one quarter of the tomato mixture with $1/2$ cup of the stock. Pulse to break down and then puree until smooth. Repeat, working in batches, until all of the sauce is pureed. Pass through a medium strainer into a clean bowl and set aside.

Lift the chiles from their liquid and transfer to the blender along with $1/2$ cup of their soaking liquid. (It is not necessary to wash the blender.) Puree in batches, adding a little more of the water as necessary and adding the chipotle, if using, to the last batch. Strain into a clean bowl.

Heat the remaining $1/4$ cup oil in a large Dutch oven or heavy casserole over medium-high heat. Season the turkey with salt and pepper and brown about 4 minutes per side. Transfer to a plate.

Pour off the fat from the Dutch oven, leaving a thin coating on the bottom. Pour in the chile puree and cook, stirring and scraping the bottom, until thick and dark, about 5 minutes. Pour in the tomato mixture and cook until thickened, 7 to 10 minutes. Add 5 cups of the broth. Bring to a simmer and cook, partially covered, stirring occasionally, 30 to 45 minutes.

Preheat the oven to 350°F.

Stir 2 teaspoons salt and the brown sugar into the mole sauce and thin the sauce, if necessary, with additional broth. Place the browned turkey in the simmering sauce. Cover and bake until the turkey is tender, about 2 hours.

Remove the mole from the oven and spoon off and discard the fat from the top. (If time allows, refrigerate, then lift off the fat, and reheat the turkey in a 350°F oven before serving.)

Serve in the casserole, or lift out the turkey, remove the skin and bones, and tear the meat into chunks. Return to the sauce. Sprinkle sesame seeds over the top to garnish. (Leftovers may be reheated in a 350°F oven.)

Serves 6 to 8

roast duck with cherry and black peppercorn sauce

1 duck, about 5 pounds

coarse salt

2 tablespoons cracked black
  pepper

2 tablespoons sugar

Sauce

2 tablespoons cold unsalted
  butter

3 shallots, minced

3/4 cup Madeira

1/2 cup dried cherries or
  cranberries

2 cups duck or chicken stock

2 tablespoons unsulfured
  molasses

1 teaspoon coarsely ground
  black pepper

1 tablespoon cornstarch,
  dissolved in 1/4 cup cold
  water

1 teaspoon sherry vinegar

freshly ground black pepper
  to taste

We like our ducks crisp-skinned and cooked all the way through. To test for doneness, wiggle a leg joint: It should feel very loose. An alternative for drying and defatting the bird is to season generously with salt and pepper and leave overnight in the refrigerator, uncovered. With its dark brown glaze and tart fruit sauce, this makes a lovely presentation.

Pierce the duck's skin all over with a sharp kitchen fork. In a large stockpot, combine 4 quarts water, 2 tablespoons salt, the cracked black pepper, and sugar and bring to a boil. Add the duck, reduce to a simmer, and cook, uncovered, 30 minutes. Transfer the duck to a platter, let cool, and pat dry. Discard the cooking liquid.

Meanwhile, make the sauce. Melt 1 tablespoon of the butter in a medium saucepan over low heat. Cook the shallots until soft and golden. Add 1/2 cup of the Madeira and the dried cherries, bring to a simmer, and cook until reduced by one third. Then add the stock, molasses, and coarse pepper and simmer 15 minutes. Whisk in the cornstarch mixture and simmer 3 to 4 minutes, until slightly thickened. Set aside. (The sauce may be made up to 2 days ahead to this point; cover and refrigerate.)

Preheat the oven to 425°F.

Season the duck's cavity with salt and pepper. Place the duck breast side up on a rack in a shallow roasting pan and roast 15 minutes. Reduce the oven temperature to 350°F, turn the duck on one side and roast 30 minutes; then turn on its other side and roast 30 minutes longer. As the duck roasts, occasionally remove the fat from the bottom of the pan with a bulb baster. Turn the duck breast side up, sprinkle with salt, and roast about 30 minutes longer, until the juices run clear.

Place the duck on an ovenproof serving platter and keep warm in the turned-off oven while you finish the sauce. (The duck can be roasted early in the day if desired. Let cool slightly, then refrigerate. Reheat in a 300°F oven; for extra-crisp skin, place under a hot broiler for 3 to 5 minutes.)

Remove all but 1 tablespoon of fat from the roasting pan. Add the remaining ¼ cup Madeira and bring to a boil over high heat, scraping up the browned bits from the bottom of the pan. Simmer until the alcohol has evaporated and the liquid has reduced slightly, about 3 minutes. Strain the reduced pan juices into the prepared duck sauce. Bring to a simmer over medium heat and stir in the sherry vinegar. Simmer 1 to 2 minutes, then swirl in the remaining 1 tablespoon cold butter. Transfer to a sauceboat for passing at the table.

Serves 2 to 4

hot tip
PAN-TOASTING

Dried herbs, chiles, garlic, and seeds can all be toasted quickly on the stove-top to release flavorful oils and their rich, smoky fragrance. Toast each ingredient individually in a small dry pan over medium heat, tossing and shaking the pan just until its aroma is released, or until the garlic skin darkens and blisters. Stay nearby, because seeds and herbs can burn in seconds.

from the sea

spicy shrimp on pan-seared grits

4 slices bacon, thinly sliced

Pan-Seared Grits, recipe
    follows

2 teaspoons ground cumin

1 teaspoon paprika

1 teaspoon cayenné pepper

¼ teaspoon coarse salt

½ teaspoon freshly ground
    black pepper

10 to 12 ounces medium
    shrimp in the shell, washed

2 tablespoons olive oil

2 red jalapeño chiles,
    stemmed, seeded, and
    julienned

2 green jalapeño chiles,
    stemmed, seeded, and
    julienned

1 bunch scallions, thinly sliced
    on the diagonal

4 garlic cloves, thinly sliced

juice of 2 limes

We like smaller shrimp in a dish like this so we can eat their tender shells and get that extra dollop of crunchy calcium our bodies sometimes crave. With its bright red color, spicy shrimp, and crisp little cornmeal cakes, this is a sure dinner-party hit.

Fry the bacon in a large heavy skillet over medium heat until crisp. With a slotted spoon, remove the bacon and drain on paper towels, reserving the fat in the pan. Crumble the bacon.

In the same skillet, sear the grits triangles over high heat until golden on both sides. With a spatula, transfer to a platter.

Combine the cumin, paprika, cayenne, salt, and pepper in a medium bowl. Add the shrimp and toss to coat evenly.

Wipe the skillet clean and heat the olive oil over high heat. Sauté the shrimp 1 to 2 minutes. Toss in the jalapeños, scallions, garlic, and reserved bacon and cook 1 minute longer. Remove from the heat and stir in the lime juice. Scatter over the seared grits and serve.

Serves 4

pan-seared grits

3 ¹/₄ cups water

³/₄ cup instant grits

¹/₂ teaspoon coarse salt

Bring the water to a boil in a medium saucepan. Stir in the grits and salt, reduce to a simmer, and cook, covered, about 10 minutes or until all the liquid is absorbed. Remove from the heat and pour into a well buttered 8-inch square baking dish. Chill until firm.

Invert the grits to remove and cut into quarters along the diagonal to make triangles.

hot tip

HOW TO PUREE GARLIC

Look for firm, heavy heads and store in a dark, well-ventilated place. Garlic at the market is about a month old and it can be kept about two additional months before losing its flavor and turning bitter. We like to puree garlic in quantity. Break the bulbs apart and crush the cloves with the flat side of a heavy knife. Remove skins and puree in a food processor or blender with a small amount of olive oil. Pureed garlic can be refrigerated in a sealed container for a week or two.

chile crab cakes

2 large eggs

³/₄ cup sour cream

3 to 4 jalapeño chiles, stemmed,
seeded, and finely diced

1 yellow bell pepper, cored,
seeded, and finely diced

1 red bell pepper, cored,
seeded, and finely diced

¹/₂ bunch scallions, white
and light green parts only,
thinly sliced

1 celery rib, finely diced

1 teaspoon celery seeds

juice of ¹/₂ lemon

3 dashes Tabasco

³/₄ teaspoon coarse salt

¹/₂ teaspoon freshly ground
black pepper

3 whole Dungeness crabs,
cooked and meat removed
(see page 86), or 1¹/₂ pounds
crabmeat picked over for
shells and cartilage

1 cup fresh bread crumbs

2 tablespoons unsalted butter

2 tablespoons vegetable oil

Romesco Sauce, page 119, or
Pimiento Salsa, page 89, for
serving (optional)

These rich little patties are spectacular served on a bed of the Parsley and Mint Salad on page 76.

In a large bowl, lightly beat the eggs. Add the sour cream, jalapeños, bell peppers, scallions, celery, celery seed, lemon juice, Tabasco, salt, and pepper. Toss together until well mixed. Shred the crab into ³/₄-inch chunks and add, along with the bread crumbs. Gently toss to combine.

Divide the mixture into 12 portions. Shape into patties about ³/₄ inch thick and 3 inches across. Transfer to a platter, cover, and chill 1 hour.

Preheat the oven to 300°F.

Heat 1 tablespoon each of the butter and oil in a large skillet over medium-high heat. Add 6 crab cakes and sauté until golden brown on the bottom, about 3 minutes. Carefully turn, and cook until the second side is golden. Place the cooked crab cakes on a baking sheet and keep warm in the oven. Add the remaining butter and oil to the pan and sauté the remaining crab cakes. Serve immediately, with one of the sauces if desired.

Serves 6

pan-fried grouper with almonds

2 1/2 pounds grouper, red
   snapper, or orange
   roughy fillets

3/4 cup slivered unblanched
   almonds

1/2 teaspoon ground allspice

2 teaspoons ground cumin

1 1/2 teaspoons paprika

1 teaspoon freshly ground
   black pepper, plus more
   to taste

1/2 teaspoon cayenne pepper

coarse salt

1/4 cup olive oil

1/2 small bunch Italian parsley,
   leaves only, chopped

lemon wedges, for garnish

We like to serve such a simple fish as this with nothing more than lemon or lime wedges and a fresh herb salad so the attention is focused on the fish and its tasty coating.

Rinse the fillets and pat dry with paper towels. Check the fish for bones and remove with tweezers if necessary.

In a food processor, combine the almonds, allspice, cumin, paprika, black pepper, and cayenne. Pulse until the almonds are finely ground, being careful not to overprocess.

Spread the nut-spice mixture in a shallow baking dish or on a platter. Season the fish all over with salt and pepper, then dredge the fillets one at a time in the nut mixture to coat, pressing on the coating so it adheres.

Heat the olive oil in a large heavy skillet over medium-high heat. Sauté the fillets about 3 minutes per side, until lightly browned and just cooked through. With a slotted spoon or spatula, transfer to a warm platter or individual serving plates. Sprinkle with the parsley and serve with lemon wedges.

Serves 6

salmon baked in salsa verde

6 (4-ounce) salmon fillets

coarse salt and freshly ground
   black pepper

Salsa Verde

2 garlic cloves

1 poblano chile, stemmed,
   seeded, and chopped

$1/2$ bunch cilantro, leaves only,
   chopped

$1/2$ bunch Italian parsley,
   leaves only, chopped

6 scallions, white and light
   green parts only, chopped

3 Roma tomatoes, cored,
   seeded, and chopped

$1/3$ cup water

2 tablespoons fruity olive oil

1 tablespoon white wine
   vinegar

2 teaspoons dried oregano

1 teaspoon coarse salt

lemon wedges, for serving

Roasting the fish in its sauce integrates the flavors in the pan, and the cook is saved the bother of making a separate sauce.

Preheat the oven to 350°F. Season the fish all over with salt and pepper and place in an oiled baking dish.

To make the salsa, combine all of the ingredients in a blender or food processor and puree.

Pour the salsa over the fish and bake 8 to 12 minutes, until the thickest part of the fish is cooked through. Serve hot with lemon wedges and the salsa spooned on top.

Serves 6

red snapper baked in vine leaves

3 tablespoons olive oil

3 tablespoons freshly
   squeezed lemon juice

1 fennel bulb, halved lengthwise and very thinly sliced
   crosswise, leaves reserved
   and chopped

1 teaspoon coarse salt

1 teaspoon freshly ground
   black pepper

6 (6-ounce) white fish fillets,
   such as red snapper, bass,
   halibut, perch, mullet,
   or pike

about 36 large vine (grape)
   leaves packed in brine,
   well rinsed

3 (¼-inch-thick) slices lemon,
   halved

extra virgin olive oil, for
   drizzling

Grapevine leaves are available in Greek or Middle Eastern markets, where they often come packed in brine. Rinse off the brine before using—or substitute another strong leafy green, such as mustard or chard. Wrapping food always enhances flavors by sealing in juices and adding a side note of flavor from the wrapper itself.

In a large shallow ceramic or glass baking dish, combine the olive oil, lemon juice, chopped fennel leaves, salt, and pepper. Pat the fish dry with paper towels and add to the marinade, turning to coat evenly. Cover with plastic wrap and marinate in the refrigerator 15 minutes.

Preheat the oven to 400°F.

Spread 3 or 4 vine leaves on a work surface, overlapping them to form a large, sturdy wrapper. Place a few slices of fennel in the center. Cover with a fish fillet and scatter a few more slices of fennel on top. Top with a half lemon slice and drizzle with olive oil. Wrap the fish in the vine leaves and lay it, seam side down, in a large baking dish. Repeat with the remaining fillets, placing them in a single layer in the dish.

Bake 20 to 30 minutes, until the fish is opaque throughout; open one package to check for doneness. Immediately transfer to serving plates and have guests unwrap the fish at the table.

Serves 6

roasted monkfish with red pepper rouille

1 small baking potato, peeled
    and chunked

4 medium White or Red Rose
    potatoes, (unpeeled)

Rouille

$\frac{1}{2}$ cup dry white wine

$\frac{1}{2}$ roasted red bell pepper,
    peeled and seeded

6 garlic cloves

3 dashes Tabasco

1 teaspoon coarse salt

$\frac{1}{2}$ teaspoon freshly ground
    black pepper

6 tablespoons fruity olive oil

1 teaspoon white vinegar

$1\frac{1}{2}$ pounds monkfish tails
    on the bone, skin and
    membranes removed

coarse salt and freshly ground
    black pepper

1 tablespoon olive oil

1 medium onion, cut crosswise
    into $\frac{1}{2}$-inch-thick slices

2 garlic cloves, minced

2 sprigs fresh rosemary

A rustic dish like this heightens everybody's senses when you bring it right to the table in a big beautiful cast-iron pan. The red rouille is a traditional Mediterranean blended sauce of roasted peppers thickened with potato. It would look lovely in an earthenware bowl alongside the casserole.

Place all the potatoes in a medium saucepan. Generously cover with water, add a pinch of salt, and bring to a boil. Cook, uncovered, until just tender, 15 to 20 minutes. Drain and set aside to cool.

Mash the baking potato with a fork or a ricer. Cut the other potatoes into long spears.

To make the rouille, bring the wine to a simmer in a small saucepan, and reduce by half. Reserve.

In a blender or food processor, combine the roasted pepper, garlic, Tabasco, salt, pepper, olive oil, vinegar, and reserved wine. Process until smooth. Transfer to a bowl. Stir in the mashed potato a little at a time until thickened to desired consistency and set aside.

Preheat the oven to 400°F.

Season the fish all over with salt and pepper.

Heat $1\frac{1}{2}$ teaspoons of the olive oil in an ovenproof 12-inch skillet, preferably cast-iron, over medium-high heat. (Don't use a pan smaller than 12 inches, or the fish will steam, rather than roast, when you add it.) Sear the onion slices, turning once or twice, until almost charred. Separate into rings and add the garlic and rosemary. Cook, stirring frequently, 1 minute, until the garlic releases its aroma. Transfer the vegetables to a plate and wipe the pan clean.

Add the remaining $1\frac{1}{2}$ teaspoons olive oil, heat until hot, and add the monkfish tails. Sear until browned all over. Return the onion mixture to the pan along with the reserved potatoes. Season generously with salt and pepper, stir to coat evenly with the oil, and arrange so the vegetables are evenly distributed in the pan.

Transfer the skillet to the oven and roast about 15 minutes, or until the fish is cooked through and the potatoes are very tender and lightly golden. Serve with the rouille on the side.

Serves 4

hot tip

SHOPPING FOR FRESH FISH

The first, and probably the most important, consideration when shopping for fresh fish is the appearance and reputation of the market. Fish is one thing we recommend bypassing at the supermarket and instead finding the best specialty shop in your locale. Look for spotlessly clean counters and displays, counterpeople who really know their product, and a lot of foot traffic. As for the specifics:

- Whole fish should have moist skin, and any interior blood should be bright red. Clouded eyes do not necessarily indicate age.
- Fillets should be translucent, not opaque, and should glisten.
- All fish should smell clean, fresh, and not "fishy." Sticky skin or texture is a bad sign.
- Shellfish should be closed and feel heavy in the hand. Light or open shells should be tossed, along with off-smelling pieces.
- If preparing freshly caught fish, gut and bleed it immediately and then wait before cooking it. Keep the fish on ice until rigor mortis leaves the body—it can take five or six hours, or even days for a huge fish—and the flesh is no longer stiff. Fish cooked too soon has a mushy, mealy texture.
- To store fresh fish, wrap the fish in plastic and place on a rack in a small baking pan or a bowl. Then cover with ice. Don't wrap shellfish—just place it on the rack and cover with the ice. As a rule, do not keep shellfish longer than three days and whole fish or fillets longer than two days.

fish baked in salt with romesco sauce

1 (4- to 5-pound) sea bass or
red snapper, gutted but not
scaled

4 to 6 pounds coarse salt

Romesco Sauce, recipe follows

If you believe that less is best when it comes to fish cookery, you owe it to yourself to try this classic Mediterranean treatment for whole fish. The salt perfectly seals in the fish's juices without overpowering its delicate flavor.

Preheat the oven to 350°F.

Rinse the fish and pat dry. Make a 2-inch layer of salt in a large casserole or roasting pan. Using your hands, make a shallow depression for the fish. Place the fish on the salt and cover completely with additional salt. Gently pat down the salt. Cover and bake about 1 hour, until a crust is formed.

Remove from the oven and set in the center of the dinner table. Break the salt crust by tapping with the back of a chef's knife to crack. Push aside the salt crust and then the skin. Lift the fish from the bones and serve immediately with the sauce.

Serves 6

hot tip

COOKING BY EAR

Don't overlook the signals
your ears pick up while cooking.
Listen for the sounds of crackling,
sizzling, sputtering, and hissing
when you pull open an oven
door or check a sauté pan.
Chances are, if you're
greeted by the sound
of silence, your oven
or pan is not
hot enough.

romesco
sauce

2 large thick slices country bread, crusts removed and cut into $^1/_2$-inch cubes

$^1/_2$ cup red wine vinegar

$^3/_4$ cup whole blanched almonds

1 pound Roma tomatoes, cored, seeded, and roughly chopped

1 tablespoon paprika

1 teaspoon coarse salt

$^1/_2$ teaspoon freshly ground black pepper

$^3/_4$ cup fruity Spanish olive oil

Preheat the oven to 350°F.

Combine the bread and vinegar in a bowl and soak about 20 minutes.

Meanwhile, spread the almonds on a baking sheet and toast in the oven, shaking the pan occasionally, until golden, 10 to 15 minutes. Let cool.

Transfer the almonds to a food processor and process until finely ground. Add the vinegar-soaked bread with all the vinegar, the tomatoes, paprika, salt, and pepper, and puree. With the machine on, add the olive oil in a slow, steady stream and process until a smooth sauce forms. Serve at room temperature.

Makes about 1 cup

salt cod and onion casserole

1 ¹/₂ pounds dried salt cod
(bacalao)

¹/₂ medium onion, sliced, plus 4
medium onions, thinly sliced
crosswise and separated
into rings

2 bay leaves

3 to 4 medium russet potatoes

¹/₃ cup plus 2 tablespoons
fruity Spanish olive oil

6 garlic cloves, minced

1 cup dry white wine

2 cups fish stock or half clam
juice and half water

1 ¹/₂ cups heavy cream

1 cup oil-cured black olives,
pitted and coarsely chopped

¹/₂ cup fresh bread crumbs

¹/₄ cup grated Spanish
Manchego or Romano
cheese

¹/₂ teaspoon freshly ground
black pepper

2 tablespoons finely chopped
Italian parsley

Salt cod is a popular ingredient in tapas bars all over Spain. Shop for it in Italian and other ethnic markets, and look for thick fillets that are not rock-hard for the best results.

To prepare the salt cod, rinse well and soak in a large container of cold water to cover. (Cut into chunks to fit if necessary.) Refrigerate, changing the soaking water two or three times, until softened, 12 to 24 hours, depending on its age.

Drain the cod and place in a large saucepan with the sliced half-onion and the bay leaves. Pour in enough fresh cold water to cover. Bring to a boil, reduce to a simmer, and taste the water. If it's excessively salty, drain the cod, cover with fresh cold water, and bring to a simmer again. Cover and simmer until the fish is opaque and plumped, about 20 minutes. It should flake into large chunks when pressed.

Drain, pat dry, and remove and discard any bones and skin. Separate into large flakes and refrigerate. (The cod can be cooked up to 2 days in advance.)

In a large saucepan of lightly salted boiling water, cook the potatoes about 30 minutes, or until just tender. Drain and, when cool enough to handle, peel if desired, and cut into ¹/₄-inch slices.

Heat ¹/₃ cup of the olive oil in a large heavy skillet over medium heat. Add the onion rings and cook, stirring frequently, until softened but not browned, about 8 minutes. Stir in the garlic and cook about 1 minute, until the aroma of the garlic is released. Remove from the heat.

Preheat the oven to 275°F.

Pour the wine into a large saucepan and boil over medium-high heat until reduced by half. Add the fish stock and reduce by half. Then add the cream and reduce by one third; there should be about 2 cups liquid remaining. Transfer to a glass or ceramic casserole about 8 inches wide and 4 inches deep.

Spread half of the potatoes in the bottom of the casserole. Cover with half of the cod and half of the onions. Sprinkle with half of the olives. Repeat the layers with the remaining potatoes, cod, onions, and olives.

In a small bowl, combine the bread crumbs, cheese, pepper, and the remaining 2 tablespoons olive oil. Sprinkle evenly over the casserole. Bake 25 to 30 minutes, until the top is golden and crisp. If desired, place briefly under a hot broiler to crisp the topping even more. Garnish with the parsley and bring the dish to the table to serve family style.

Serves 6

brazilian seafood stew

2 tablespoons olive oil

1 medium onion, diced

1 red bell pepper, cored, seeded, and diced

1 green bell pepper, cored, seeded, and diced

1 yellow bell pepper, cored, seeded, and diced

2 Roma tomatoes, cored, seeded, and diced

1 1/2 serrano chiles, stemmed, seeded, and minced

2 teaspoons coarse salt, plus more to taste

1 teaspoon freshly ground black pepper, plus more to taste

3 cups fish stock or clam juice

1 (14 1/2-ounce) can coconut milk

3/4 pound sea scallops

3/4 pound monkfish fillet, cut into 1-inch cubes

3/4 pound rock shrimp, shelled and deveined

6 scallions, white and light green parts only, thinly sliced

Jack Harding, a former sous chef at City restaurant, showed us this typical seafood stew from Brazil. It derives its unusual flavor from coconut and dendê oil, a Brazilian palm oil, available in Latin American markets. Be sure to get the Brazilian rather than the West African product, since it is lighter.

Heat the olive oil in a large heavy pot or Dutch oven over low heat. Add the onion and bell peppers and cook about 5 minutes, or until nicely softened. Stir in the tomatoes, chiles, salt and pepper and cook about 2 minutes more. Pour in the fish stock and coconut milk and bring to a boil over medium-high heat. Reduce to a simmer and cook 10 to 15 minutes, stirring occasionally, until the peppers are tender.

Season all the seafood with salt and pepper. Add to the pot, along with the scallions, cover, and simmer 5 to 7 minutes, gently stirring twice. Add the lime juice, dendê oil, and cilantro and simmer 2 minutes longer. Ladle into large bowls and garnish with the toasted coconut strips and the limes. Serve with fried plantains and white rice on the side if desired.

Serves 6

juice of 1 lime

2 tablespoons dendê oil
(optional)

$1/3$ cup loosely packed cilantro
leaves, coarsely chopped

$1/3$ cup Chile-Toasted Coconut
Strips, page 8, for garnish

2 limes, peel and pits removed,
separated into sections,
and diced, for garnish

fried plantains, for serving
(optional)

white rice, for serving
(optional)

hot tip

SEASONING IN STAGES

A well-seasoned, well-cooked dish should be seasoned
(and tasted) every step of the way, not just at the end. If you
save the seasonings for the end, their flavors will remain on the
surface, more like an afterthought than an integrated part of the dish.
But when you season carefully in stages, the flavors keep intermingling,
resulting in a more thorough marriage.

We always season foods before marinating, grilling, or broiling. In a
sauté, we begin seasoning with the onions and don't stop until the final
adjustment. And in our soups and stews, the stocks are seasoned, the
aromatics and meats are seasoned, even the garnishes are seasoned.

The best way to make seasoning a way of life is to keep a bowl
of coarse salt and a peppermill near the stove. Using your
fingertips to add salt, rather than sprinkling it from a
shaker, gives you much better control.

from the field

potato cake

2 pounds russet potatoes,
   peeled if desired

1 teaspoons coarse salt

$^{1}/_{2}$ teaspoon freshly ground
   black pepper

$^{1}/_{2}$ cup olive oil

2 large onions, thinly sliced

6 large eggs

In Spain, it is not unusual to see four or five varieties of this traditional potato cake, or tortilla, cut into small wedges and served as tapas in bars. Typical additions are asparagus, tuna, and mayonnaise. We love it plain, as part of a vegetarian meal, served alongside dishes like our Artichoke Stew with Pine Nuts (page 126) or Swiss Chard with Roasted Garlic (page 165). It's also a wonderful make-ahead addition to any brunch menu.

Halve the potatoes lengthwise and, with a sharp knife, a mandoline, or a food processor, cut crosswise into $^{1}/_{16}$-inch-thick slices. Toss the potatoes with $^{1}/_{2}$ teaspoon of the salt and $^{1}/_{4}$ teaspoon of the pepper.

Heat $^{1}/_{4}$ cup of the olive oil in a 9-inch cast-iron skillet over medium heat. Add the potatoes and cook, tossing occasionally with a spatula, until golden and crisp, 10 to 15 minutes; do not worry if they stick a bit. Remove the potatoes from the pan with a slotted spoon and drain for a moment on paper towels. Wipe out the pan with a paper towel and set aside.

Meanwhile, heat 2 tablespoons of the olive oil in medium skillet over medium-low heat. Sauté the onions, stirring occasionally, about 20 minutes, until very soft and slightly golden. Remove from the heat and let cool slightly.

Preheat the oven to 350°F.

In a large bowl, beat the eggs. Stir in the onions and the remaining $^{1}/_{2}$ teaspoon salt and $^{1}/_{4}$ teaspoon pepper.

Add the remaining 2 tablespoons oil to the potato skillet and heat over low heat. Stir the potatoes into the egg mixture, and immediately scrape into the hot skillet. Cook about 8 minutes, or until the bottom of the cake is slightly golden. Place a large plate upside down over the skillet, invert, and turn the cake out onto the plate. Slide the cake back into the pan, cooked side up, and transfer to the oven. Bake 4 to 5 minutes, until the eggs are set. Cool in the pan 5 minutes, then cut into wedges, or into small squares for tapas, and serve warm (or at room temperature—also wonderful).

Serves 6 as an entrée, 10 as a tapa

Variation: Add 2 peeled and diced roasted red peppers and 1 tablespoon paprika to the onion mixture before combining it with the eggs.

hot tip

SLICING AND DICING WITH THE CHEFS

· Place anything to be cut on a cutting board. Never cut into the air or toward your body.
· With fruits and vegetables, create a flat side first. Take a slice off round vegetables and fruits, such as melons and oranges, then lay on the counter and slice.
· When cutting a fruit or vegetable with a tough skin, like a bell pepper, halve, then cut from the flesh side, because the tough skin will dull the blade.
· Hold the item being cut with a hand with curled-back fingers, so your fingers, between the first and second knuckle, guide the blade while your thumb inches the item forward.

artichoke stew with pine nuts

½ cup red wine vinegar

6 cups water

36 baby artichokes (about 4 to 5 pounds)

6 slices bacon, finely diced (optional)

1 tablespoon olive oil

1 large onion, finely chopped

3 garlic cloves, minced

1 pound ripe tomatoes, cored, peeled, seeded, and chopped

3 cups vegetable stock or water

1½ teaspoons coarse salt, or more to taste

½ teaspoon freshly ground black pepper, or more to taste

¼ cup toasted pine nuts

juice of 1 lemon

If you are an artichoke lover as Susan is, here is an opportunity to perfume an entire dish with the heady aroma of tender baby artichokes. Build a meal around this stew by serving rice or potatoes and a crunchy salad alongside.

Combine the vinegar and water in a large glass or ceramic bowl. Slice and discard about ½ inch from the top of each artichoke and trim the stems. Remove and discard the outer leaves and remove any sharp points with scissors. Cut the artichokes in half and reserve in the vinegar mixture.

In a large enameled saucepan, cook the bacon over medium-low heat until golden. Remove with a slotted spoon and drain on paper towels. Drain off all but 1½ tablespoons of the fat from the pan, and add the olive oil. Add the onion and cook until softened, about 5 minutes. Then add the garlic and cook 2 minutes longer, just to release its aroma. Add the tomatoes, turn the heat to medium, and cook until the pan is nearly dry, 10 to 15 minutes.

Pour in the stock, add the bacon, salt, and pepper and bring to a boil. Drain the artichokes well and add to the pan. Reduce to a simmer and cook, covered, about 15 minutes. Stir in the pine nuts and cook another 15 minutes, or until the artichokes are tender. Adjust the seasonings with salt, pepper, and lemon juice and serve hot.

Serves 6

hot tip

ON ARTICHOKES

The best time for artichokes is spring and summer, when the farmers in Castroville, the artichoke center of California, and possibly the world, are harvesting them by the bushelful. We never can resist them in the market. Here is what to look for: Large artichokes should feel heavy and solid in the hand. When the leaves are rubbed together, they should squeak. Avoid brown ones and/or any that feel light and hollow—all signs of toughness. We are partial to the small baby ones that show up at farmers' markets in the spring. The smallest, most tender ones can be eaten raw: Simply slice thin and drizzle with olive oil and salt for a traditional Italian salad. Or add to stews and braises after trimming the stems, cutting off the top ½ inch of each one, and cutting in half if desired.

pisto
manchego

1 medium eggplant,
   (unpeeled), cut into
   large cubes

coarse salt

$1/2$ cup olive oil

3 medium zucchini, cut into
   large cubes

2 large onions, coarsely
   chopped

3 green bell peppers, cored,
   seeded, and cut into large
   squares

6 medium tomatoes, cored,
   seeded, and coarsely
   chopped

freshly ground black pepper

1 large egg, lightly beaten

This simple Spanish vegetable stew is similar to a French ratatouille, with an added dollop of richness from the egg that is stirred in at the end. The egg binds the juices with the vegetables and gives an otherwise rustic stew a smooth, luxurious texture. It would be delicious on squares of grilled polenta or tossed with pasta as a sauce.

Place the eggplant in a colander set on a plate, sprinkle evenly with salt, and let sit 30 minutes. Pat dry.

Heat 3 tablespoons of the olive oil in a large heavy skillet over medium-high heat. Sauté the eggplant until golden. Transfer to paper towels to drain. Add 2 more tablespoons oil to the pan and sauté the zucchini until golden. Transfer to paper towels to drain.

Add the onions and cook 5 minutes. Then add the bell peppers and cook, stirring occasionally, until caramelized, about 10 minutes. Push the onion mixture to the edges of the pan and pour in the remaining 3 tablespoons oil. Add the tomatoes and 1 teaspoon salt, reduce the heat to medium, and cook about 5 minutes, until the tomatoes soften a bit.

Return all of the vegetables to the pan, reduce the heat to medium-low, and cook, covered, about 10 minutes. Remove from heat and season with salt and pepper. Stir in the beaten egg and cook just until barely set.

Serves 6

peruvian vegetable stew

2 tablespoons unsalted butter

1 teaspoon cayenne pepper

1 ear corn, shucked and cut
into $\frac{1}{2}$-inch slices

juice of $\frac{1}{2}$ lime

$\frac{1}{4}$ cup olive oil

2 medium onions, finely
chopped

3 large garlic cloves, finely
chopped

2 medium butternut squash
(about $3\frac{1}{2}$ pounds), peeled,
seeded, and cut into 1-inch
chunks

2 large tomatoes, cored,
seeded, and chopped

$\frac{1}{2}$ small bunch oregano,
leaves only, coarsely
chopped

2 teaspoons coarse salt, or
more to taste

1 teaspoon freshly ground
black pepper, or more
to taste

4 cups water

$1\frac{1}{4}$ cups fresh corn kernels

1 cup fresh or thawed
frozen peas

Disks of sweet and spicy corn in the cob distinguish this traditional stew. It makes great use of winter squash and two of our favorite frozen vegetables—peas and corn. So when the winter dinner doldrums get you down, lift your spirits with this splendidly fresh-tasting one-dish-meal.

Melt the butter in a medium skillet over medium-high heat. Stir in the cayenne and corn slices and cook about 2 minutes per side, until golden and evenly coated with the cayenne. Add the lime juice and turn the corn to coat evenly. Remove from the heat and set aside.

Heat the olive oil in a large skillet over medium heat. Sauté the onions 7 to 8 minutes, or until slightly golden. Add the garlic and cook 1 minute longer, or until its aroma is released. Add the squash, tomatoes, oregano, salt, pepper, and water. Stir to combine and cook, stirring occasionally, about 25 minutes, or until the squash is nearly tender.

Stir in the corn kernels and peas, cover, and cook 5 minutes longer. Taste for seasoning and serve, garnished with the sautéed corn slices.

Serves 6

baked chiles stuffed with corn

Here is a lighter, all-vegetable-and-cheese alternative to chiles rellenos.

4 tablespoons unsalted butter
  or ¼ cup vegetable oil

1 medium onion, chopped

2 garlic cloves, minced

3 cups fresh or thawed frozen
  corn kernels

1½ teaspoons coarse salt

1 teaspoon freshly ground
  black pepper

½ cup grated Mexican
  Manchego or Monterey
  Jack cheese

½ cup grated panela or
  farmer's cheese

½ cup grated añejo or
  Romano cheese

3 tablespoons chopped fresh
  epazote or oregano

6 large poblano chiles, roasted
  and carefully peeled without
  tearing

4 cups cooked white rice

1 cup Crema, page 186, or
  heavy cream

1 cup milk

Preheat the oven to 350°F.

Melt the butter in a medium saucepan over medium heat. Sauté the onion 5 to 6 minutes until softened. Add the garlic and cook 1 minute more, or until its aroma is released. Add the corn, salt, and pepper and sauté until tender, 2 to 3 minutes. Transfer to a bowl and let cool, then stir in the cheeses and epazote and set aside.

Carefully slit the chiles lengthwise and remove the seeds and veins, leaving the stems and tops intact if possible. Stuff the chiles with the corn mixture.

Spread the rice in a shallow baking pan or casserole. Nestle the chiles in the rice, in a single layer. Pour the crema and milk over all and transfer to the oven. Bake 15 to 20 minutes, until heated through. Serve hot.

Serves 6

peruvian egg noodles

Noodles

9 large eggs

1 teaspoon coarse salt

$^{1}/_{2}$ teaspoon freshly ground
   black pepper

$^{1}/_{4}$ cup grated Mexican
   Manchego cheese

$^{1}/_{4}$ cup finely crushed water
   biscuits

1 tablespoon unsalted butter,
   melted

Tomato Sauce

3 tablespoons olive oil

1 medium onion, chopped

2 large garlic cloves, minced

2 teaspoons ground fennel

1 teaspoon paprika

1 teaspoon cayenne pepper

coarse salt and freshly ground
   black pepper

4 cups chopped canned
   tomatoes

1 small carrot, peeled and
   grated

$^{1}/_{2}$ small bunch fresh basil,
   leaves only, coarsely
   chopped, for garnish

Don't let the name fool you. The lovely golden noodles in this dish are actually thin ribbons of omelet tossed in a quick tomato sauce. This is a great choice for brunch, since it is delicious served at room temperature.

Combine the eggs, salt, and pepper in a large bowl. Whisk together until evenly blended, then stir in the grated cheese and crushed biscuits.

Lightly brush a medium nonstick skillet with the butter and place over medium heat. Pour enough of the eggs into the pan to form a thin layer and quickly swirl to coat evenly. Cook until set, about $1^{1}/_{2}$ minutes. Using a long wide spatula, turn the omelet and cook a few seconds more. Slide onto a plate and continue making omelets until all the eggs are cooked. Stack the omelets—you should have about eight— cover, and keep warm.

Heat the olive oil in a large heavy casserole over low heat. Cook the onion, stirring occasionally, about 7 minutes, or until translucent. Stir in the garlic, fennel, paprika, cayenne pepper, and salt and pepper to taste. Cook 2 minutes longer, until the garlic releases its aroma. Add the tomatoes and carrot, increase the heat to medium-high, and cook until most of the liquid has evaporated, about 8 minutes. Remove from the heat.

Tightly roll the omelets (in two batches, if necessary) into a cylinder and cut crosswise into ¼-inch-wide strips. Transfer the strips to the hot tomato sauce and toss over low heat to heat through. Garnish with the chopped basil and serve in pasta bowls.

Serves 4 to 6

vegetarian black bean chili

2 cups dried black beans, rinsed, picked over, and soaked overnight

6 cups water, or more as needed

1 cup beer

¼ cup olive oil

2 small red onions, diced

coarse salt and freshly ground black pepper

1 green bell pepper, cored, seeded, and cut into ½-inch cubes

2 ribs celery, coarsely chopped

1 medium carrot, coarsely chopped

2 zucchini, diced

1 red bell pepper, cored, seeded, and diced

1 yellow bell pepper, cored, seeded, and diced

4 large garlic cloves, coarsely chopped

3 tablespoons white wine vinegar

We each love to entertain casually in our homes. Serve a great chili like this one directly from the stovetop to set the tone and keep the party flowing. Just set the pot over a low flame, arrange the garnishes in bowls in the kitchen, and toss together a big green salad. All you need are unlimited cold beers and warm tortillas to complete the mood.

Drain the beans and rinse under cold running water. In a large soup pot, combine the beans with the water and bring to a boil, skimming and discarding any scum that rises to the top.

Add the beer and return to a boil. Reduce to a simmer and cook, covered, 45 minutes to 1 hour, until the beans are tender but not falling apart: check occasionally and add water if necessary to keep the beans covered. Drain in a colander, reserving the cooking liquid.

Meanwhile, heat the olive oil in a large Dutch oven over medium-low heat. Add the red onions and salt and pepper to taste and cook 6 to 8 minutes, until caramelized. Add the green pepper, celery, and carrot and cook about 5 minutes, stirring occasionally, until softened. Add the zucchini and red and yellow bell peppers and cook about 10 minutes longer, until all the vegetables are nicely softened. Add the garlic and cook about 2 minutes, until the aroma is released.

Stir in 3 cups of the reserved bean cooking liquid, the vinegar, half of the parsley, and the spice mix and bring to a simmer. Cover and simmer about 30 minutes, stirring occasionally.

Add the drained black beans, the tomatoes, corn, and lemon juice and cook 15 more minutes. Stir in the remaining parsley and serve, with the garnishes in bowls for adding at the table.

Serves 6 to 8

1 small bunch Italian parsley,
  leaves only, coarsely
  chopped

¼ cup Chile Powder Mix,
  recipe follows

1 (12-ounce) can plum
  tomatoes, cut into 1-inch
  cubes

1 cup fresh or thawed frozen
  corn kernels

Juice of 1 lemon

Garnishes

Crema, page 186, or sour
  cream

1 cup grated Monterey
  Jack cheese

4 scallions, thinly sliced

hot tip

BEAN COOKERY

When cooking any dried bean, always cook with the lid on and
never salt the water. Salt will toughen the beans' skins.
To test for doneness, taste a few of the smallest beans.
If their centers are smooth and creamy, not powdery,
the beans are done. Since dried beans can be too old,
try to shop for beans at a market where there is
quick turnover. In our travels in some Latin
American countries, we learned that beans are
dated for freshness and that beans older than
one year are removed from the shelves.

chile powder mix

Mix the ingredients together and store in a sealed jar.

3 tablespoons ancho chile
   powder

Makes $^1/_2$ cup

1 tablespoon ground cumin

2 teaspoons dried oregano,
   crumbled

1 teaspoon ground coriander

1 teaspoon freshly ground
   black pepper

1 teaspoon coarse salt

hot tip

BROWN IS THE FLAVOR WE LOVE

Before adding grains to a stew, soup, or pilaf, we love to develop their flavors by toasting—a technique called rissole in France. Heat a vegetable oil with a high burning point, or butter, in a skillet, toss in the grain, and sauté until the grains begin to color slightly. Pour in the stock, cover, and slowly cook that deep toasted flavor into the broth.

baked
fideo

2 pounds Roma tomatoes,
   cored and halved

1 large onion, roughly chopped

8 garlic cloves, halved

$^1/_2$ cup water

2 teaspoons coarse salt

$^1/_2$ cup olive oil

12 ounces fideo, vermicelli,
   or angel hair pasta, broken
   into 1-inch pieces

6 dried chipotle chiles

2 cups vegetable stock or
   water

$^3/_4$ cup grated añejo cheese

Garnishes

1 avocado, halved, seeded,
   peeled, and cut into 8
   wedges

1 small bunch cilantro, leaves
   only, chopped

Crema, page 186, or sour
   cream (optional)

We are huge fans of the traditional *sopas secas,* or dried soups, of Mexico. With just a few simple ingredients from the pantry, you can make a dish of unusual depth. Stir leftover baked fideo into chicken stock and garnish with lime and avocado for an instant Mexican soup.

In a blender, combine the tomatoes, onion, garlic, water, and salt. Puree until smooth. Set aside. Preheat the oven to 350°F. Lightly oil a 13 × 9-inch baking dish.

Heat the olive oil in a large heavy saucepan over medium-low heat. Add the broken pasta and sauté, stirring frequently to avoid burning, until deep golden brown. Add the chiles and cook, stirring, 2 minutes longer. Stir in the tomato puree and the stock or water and bring to a simmer. Pour into the baking dish.

Cover with aluminum foil and bake 10 to 15 minutes, until all the liquid has been absorbed and the noodles are tender. Uncover and sprinkle the cheese over the top. Turn the oven temperature up to 400°F and bake, uncovered, an additional 10 minutes, or until bubbling and golden. Arrange the avocado slices on top, sprinkle with the cilantro, drizzle with the crema if desired, and serve.

Serves 6 to 8

Variation: Sauté 1 pound mushrooms, sliced, with 1 onion finely diced, and 1 small bunch epazote, leaves only, in olive oil and stir into the fideo mixture before baking.

crispy-bottomed basmati rice with lentils

3 cups basmati rice

2 tablespoons plus 1 teaspoon coarse salt

$^1/_4$ cup fruity olive oil

1 large onion, diced

2 cups brown lentils, picked over, rinsed, and drained

4 to 5 garlic cloves, minced

1 teaspoon Hungarian paprika

1 teaspoon freshly ground black pepper

3 cups water

1 bunch fresh basil, leaves only, julienned

We are always happy to place two grains at the center of the meal. Mary Sue has been working on perfecting this impressive Persian dish, called a *tadik,* since she first learned of it twelve years ago from her husband, Josh. Serve with roasted and marinated red bell peppers for a complete, and lovely, vegetarian meal.

Wash the rice in several changes of cold water, until the water runs clear. Transfer to a large bowl, add cold water to cover and 1 tablespoon of the salt, and soak at least 8 hours, or overnight.

Heat 2 tablespoons of the oil in a large skillet over medium heat. Sauté the onion until translucent, about 10 minutes. Add the lentils, garlic, paprika, and pepper and cook 2 minutes. Add the water, cover, and simmer until the lentils are tender, about 1 hour.

Season the lentils with 1 teaspoon of the salt, stir in the basil, and set aside.

In a large saucepan, combine 2½ quarts of water and the remaining 1 tablespoon salt and bring to a boil. Drain the rice and add to the saucepan. Bring back to a boil and cook, uncovered, 6 to 8 minutes. The rice should be about three-quarters done—the outsides soft and the centers still firm. Drain in a colander and rinse well with warm water. Drain well.

Heat the remaining 2 tablespoons oil in a 10- to 12-inch heavy pot over medium heat. Sprinkle in about 2 tablespoons of water. A spoonful at a time, sprinkle about two thirds of the rice evenly over the bottom of the pot. Spread the lentil mixture evenly over the rice. Cover with the remaining rice, mounding it slightly in the center.

Using the handle of a wooden spoon, poke about 5 holes in the rice, down to the bottom of the pot, to allow steam to escape. Cover with a thick dish towel and then a tight-fitting lid. Cook over medium-low heat, turning the pot occasionally, 35 to 40 minutes, until the rice begins to turn golden on the bottom.

To unmold, fill the sink with 1 to 2 inches of cold water. Have a large round platter nearby. Uncover the pot and place in the sink for a minute. Remove, dry off the bottom, and invert the beautiful golden-brown rice cake onto the serving platter. Cut into wedges to serve.

Serves 6

hot tip
HOW TO RINSE RICE

As rice is transported, the grains knock against one another, forming a sort of rice "flour" coating on all the grains. This is what causes gumminess in cooked rice. We always remove the starch by rinsing before cooking. Place the rice in the bottom of a large bowl under a gently flowing stream of cold water. Keep stirring with your hand to loosen these fine particles and drain off the cloudy water. Continue rinsing until the water runs clear.

from the range

spicy rabbit stew

1 bunch Italian parsley

4 cups chicken stock,
    preferably homemade

4 cups water

1 ($1^{1}/_{2}$-inch) piece fresh ginger
    (unpeeled), cut into thick
    slices

2 whole heads garlic
    (unpeeled), halved
    crosswise, plus 3 large
    garlic cloves, minced

6 jalapeño chiles

1 tablespoon annatto seeds

2 teaspoons juniper berries

1 tablespoon black pepper-
    corns, cracked

1 tablespoon coarse salt,
    or more to taste

1 rabbit (about $3^{1}/_{2}$ pounds),
    rinsed, patted dry, and cut
    into serving pieces

$^{1}/_{4}$ cup olive oil

1 cup orzo pasta

1 medium onion, minced

Stewing and braising are the best methods for cooking rabbit because it benefits from long, slow cooking. In this delicious stew, inspired by the Peruvian kitchen, we stretch an expensive ingredient with starchy orzo and peas so that one little rabbit serves as many as eight. This is a great one-dish winter meal with a baguette and salad.

Remove the leaves from half the parsley, finely chop, and set aside. Combine the chicken stock, water, ginger, heads of garlic, the remaining parsley, the jalapeños, annatto seeds, juniper berries, peppercorns, and 2 teaspoons of the salt in a large stockpot. Bring to a boil, reduce to a simmer, and cook, partially covered, skimming and discarding any foam from the top, 15 minutes.

Add the rabbit. Bring back to a simmer and cook about 1 hour and 15 minutes, until the meat is tender: Cooking times will vary for each part, so test several times for doneness and remove each when tender, transferring to a plate with tongs. When cool enough to handle, remove the meat from the bones and cut into large chunks. Discard the bones and set the meat aside.

Strain the stock through a colander, pressing against the vegetables to extract as much flavor as possible, and then strain again through a fine sieve. If necessary, add water so the liquid equals 8 cups.

In a large heavy casserole, heat the olive oil over high heat. Add the orzo and cook, stirring constantly, until golden,

1 tablespoon paprika

1 tablespoon achiote paste
(see page 145) mashed with
2 tablespoons water

2 cups fresh or thawed
frozen peas

about 4 minutes. Add the onion, garlic cloves, and the remaining 1 teaspoon salt and cook 1 minute more, until the aroma of the garlic is released. Add the paprika and the achiote paste mixture, mashing it well with the back of a spoon, and cook 1 minute more. Pour in the reserved stock and bring to a simmer.

Simmer, stirring and scraping the bottom occasionally to prevent scorching, about 30 minutes. Add the rabbit with its juices and the peas and cook 5 minutes longer. Adjust the seasoning, garnish with the reserved parsley, and serve in bowls.

Serves 6 to 8

hot tip

POTS AND PANS

When we shop for pots and pans, we take two factors into consideration: weight and conductability. The best pans are heavy and made of good conductors like iron, aluminum, or copper. At the restaurant, our pots are almost exclusively aluminum, because they are inexpensive, light enough, and heat evenly. (We have learned that aluminum is probably not a health hazard, as was thought a few years back.) At home, of course, appearance counts more, as does ease of care. These days we are partial to big enameled cast-iron casseroles with handles on both sides for bringing to the table and the heavier high-quality nonstick pans that allow us to use less fat and clean up so easily.

pork chops with prunes and pine nuts

Stuffing

12 ounces pitted prunes,

$^3/_4$ cup port wine

1 tablespoon olive oil

$^1/_4$ cup pine nuts

$^1/_2$ teaspoon coarse salt

$^1/_4$ teaspoon freshly ground
black pepper

6 thick-cut bone-in loin pork
chops (about 8 ounces each)

1 teaspoon coarse salt

$^1/_2$ teaspoon freshly ground
black pepper

1 tablespoon olive oil

6 medium shallots, minced

$^1/_4$ cup port wine

1$^1/_2$ cups beef stock

2 tablespoons unsalted butter,
cut into 4 pieces

juice of $^1/_2$ lemon

Stuffed pork chops always make an impressive entrée for a dinner party. Match these with the Mimosa Salad (page 77), some potatoes or rice, and a fabulous dessert for a special-occasion feast.

To make the stuffing, combine the prunes with the port in a medium saucepan. Bring to a boil, reduce to a simmer, and cook, uncovered, 10 to 15 minutes. Drain, reserving the liquid. Roughly chop the prunes and set aside.

Heat the olive oil in a medium skillet over medium heat. Sauté the pine nuts, stirring frequently, 1 to 2 minutes, until golden. Stir in the prunes and the reserved port. Continue cooking, stirring occasionally, until the liquid is reduced to a glaze. Stir in the salt and pepper and let cool.

To stuff the chops, cut each in half horizontally, almost to the bone, to create a pocket. Loosely stuff the chops, reserving any leftover stuffing. Secure the edges of each chop with two toothpicks. Season with the salt and pepper.

Preheat the oven to 350°F, and place a roasting pan in it to heat.

Heat a large heavy well-seasoned skillet (or two smaller pans) over high heat until very hot. Sear the chops about 1$^1/_2$ minutes per side. Transfer the chops to the roasting pan in the oven and bake 15 to 20 minutes, until done.

Meanwhile, add the olive oil to the skillet and place over medium-high heat. Sauté the shallots 6 to 8 minutes, until golden. Pour in the port and simmer until reduced by half. Add the beef stock and reduce again by half. Add any leftover filling. Increase the heat to high and reduce until thickened to taste. Reduce the heat and stir in the butter and lemon juice until the sauce is smooth.

Spoon the sauce over the chops and serve immediately.

Serves 6

spanish bean stew with sausages

Salsa Verde

¹/₂ bunch Italian parsley, leaves only, finely chopped

¹/₂ small white onion, finely diced

1 tablespoon capers, rinsed and coarsely chopped

1 teaspoon coarse salt, or to taste

¹/₂ teaspoon freshly ground black pepper

2¹/₂ tablespoons sherry vinegar

¹/₄ cup fruity Spanish olive oil

1 pound large white beans, rinsed, picked over, and soaked overnight in water to cover generously

1 tablespoon olive oil

4 slices bacon, thinly sliced

4 onions, sliced

1 pound leeks, white parts only, washed and sliced

1 large carrot, peeled and coarsely chopped

12 large garlic cloves, minced

1 tablespoon paprika

2 ham hocks

2 bay leaves

4 cups water

1 pound hot-smoked linguiça sausage, cut into 1-inch chunks

coarse salt and freshly ground black pepper

Like cassoulet or red beans and rice, this traditional Spanish stew is a slow blend of two deep, rich ingredients—beans and smoked meats. The piquant salsa introduces acidity to balance the heartiness.

To make the salsa, in a bowl, whisk together the parsley, onion, capers, salt, pepper, vinegar and olive oil. Cover with plastic wrap and refrigerate up to 24 hours.

Drain the beans.

Heat the oil in a very large enameled cast-iron or other heavy casserole over medium heat. Cook the bacon 3 to 4 minutes, until most of the fat is rendered. Remove all but 1 tablespoon of the fat and discard.

Add the onions and sauté until golden. Stir in the leeks and carrot and continue cooking, stirring occasionally, 10 minutes, or until all the vegetables are very soft. Add the garlic and cook 5 minutes longer, or until soft but not browned. Add the paprika and cook 1 to 2 minutes to release its aroma.

Add the ham hocks, bay leaves, beans, and water and bring to a boil, skimming and discarding the scum that rises to the surface. Reduce to a simmer and cook, partially covered, 1 hour; add more water as necessary.

Add the sausage and cook 30 minutes more, or until the beans are tender.

Lift out the ham hocks and remove and discard the rind and fat. Shred the meat and return to the pot. Remove and discard the bay leaves. Add salt and pepper to taste and serve in bowls, with a small spoonful of the salsa verde topping each one.

Serves 6 to 8

barbecued ribs with red chile sauce and baked pineapple

Red Chile Sauce

4 ounces ancho chiles, wiped
   clean, stemmed, and seeded

2 cups boiling water

8 large garlic cloves, peeled

$^1/_2$ cup molasses

3 tablespoons red wine
   vinegar

$^1/_2$ cup Dijon mustard

1 tablespoon dried oregano

1 $^1/_2$ teaspoons coarse salt

1 teaspoon freshly ground
   black pepper

$^1/_4$ cup honey

juice of 1 lime

4 $^1/_2$ pounds pork baby back or
   country-style ribs

Baked Pineapple,
   recipe follows

These supremely messy, sticky, brick-red ribs are a snap to make—simply marinate and bake. Mary Sue recommends country-style ribs and also suggests trying the sauce on grilled chicken. Pineapple is a traditional counterpoint to savory pork, and, baked in its skin, it retains all its juices.

To make the chile sauce, cover the chiles with the boiling water. Soak until softened, about 10 minutes.

Transfer the chiles with their liquid and the garlic to a blender. Puree about 1 minute, scraping down the sides with a rubber spatula. Add the molasses, vinegar, mustard, oregano, salt, and pepper. Blend until smooth. (The chile sauce may be made ahead and refrigerated up to 2 weeks.)

Put the ribs in a glass or ceramic dish, and rub them all over with salt and pepper and then with 1 cup of the chile sauce. Cover and marinate in the refrigerator 2 to 4 hours, or overnight.

Preheat the oven to 350°F.

Lift the ribs from the marinade and place in a single layer in a baking pan. Cover and refrigerate the marinade. Add water to the baking pan to a depth of ½ inch. Bake, uncovered, 45 minutes. Cover the pan with foil and bake an additional 30 minutes. Test for doneness by piercing between the ribs with a kitchen fork: The ribs should slide off the fork. Remove the ribs from the pan and set aside. Pour the juices from the baking pan into a small saucepan and add reserved marinade honey and lime juice. Briefly simmer to thicken for glaze.

Finish the ribs either in a 450°F oven or on a hot grill: Bake 10 minutes per side, brushing with glaze every 5 minutes, or grill 5 minutes per side, frequently brushing with glaze. Cut the ribs apart and serve hot with the baked pineapple.

Serves 4

baked pineapple

1 ripe pineapple, leaves
  removed

1 lime, quartered

1 ½ teaspoons cayenne
  pepper, or to taste

1 tablespoon finely chopped
  fresh Italian parsley

Preheat the oven to 350°F. Place the whole pineapple in a roasting pan and bake about 1 hour. Set aside to cool.

When it is cool enough to handle, cut the pineapple crosswise into 8 thick rounds. Halve the slices and arrange on a platter. Squeeze the lime juice over the pineapple, dust with cayenne pepper, and sprinkle with the chopped parsley.

hot tip

ON PINEAPPLES

We recommend baby pineapples, if you can find them, because they are invariably riper and tastier than the larger ones. Pineapples stop ripening once they are off the tree, so although they will soften they will not sweeten. To shop for a sweet pineapple, pull out a leaf and sniff the leaf tip from the fruit end, or press and smell the bottom end. Both should smell sweet. Also, look for pineapples that are gold, not green.

cochinita pibil

1/2 cup achiote paste or annatto seeds

10 garlic cloves, chopped

1 1/2 cups orange juice

juice of 2 limes

8 bay leaves, crumbled

2 teaspoons cumin seeds

2 teaspoons dried thyme

1 teaspoon dried oregano

1/2 teaspoon ground cinnamon

1 teaspoon coarse salt

2 teaspoons freshly ground black pepper

4 pounds pork butt, cut into 3-inch cubes

2 white onions, sliced crosswise 1/2 inch thick

5 Roma tomatoes, cored and sliced 1/2 inch thick

1 pound banana leaves, softened over low heat (optional)

4 Anaheim chiles, roasted, peeled, seeded, and sliced into strips

Pickled Shallots, page 79, for serving

Traditional pibil cooking from Mexico's Yucatán Peninsula calls for marinating little pigs (*cochinitas*) in a blend of achiote paste, citrus, and spices before wrapping them in fragrant banana leaves and lowering them into a carefully built banana leaf–lined pit called a *pibe*. Here is our adaptation for the American kitchen of a dish we first tasted in Playa del Carmen.

In a medium bowl, mash together the achiote paste, garlic, orange juice, lime juice, bay leaves, cumin, thyme, oregano, cinnamon, salt, and pepper with a fork. Add the pork, toss to coat evenly, and marinate at room temperature at least 4 hours.

Preheat the oven to 300°F.

Heat a dry cast-iron skillet over high heat. Char the onion slices until blackened on both sides. Set aside, then char the tomato slices on both sides. Set aside.

Line a large baking dish with a layer of banana leaves, or line it with foil. Arrange the pork in an even layer and top with the onions, tomatoes, chiles, and all the marinade. Cover with more banana leaves and wrap the dish tightly in foil.

Bake 2 1/2 to 3 hours, or until the pork is tender but still moist. Remove from the oven and let sit 10 minutes. Serve with the pickled shallots.

Serves 8 to 10

hot tip

ACHIOTE PASTE

Achiote paste is a bright orange seasoning paste from the Yucatán made of ground annatto seeds, oregano, cumin, cinnamon, pepper, and cloves. It is often thinned with vinegar or citrus juices for marinades and sauces. Cooking enhances the flavor greatly and removes any chalkiness. It's achiote paste that produces the bright orange color often found in Mexican food, so be sure to wear an apron and wash off any utensils that touch it as soon as possible, or they just might remain orange. (Annatto seeds are sometimes used to color Cheddar cheese!) The paste is sold in bricks in Mexican markets and can be kept, well wrapped, in the refrigerator for a long time

stew that stains the tablecloth

When Los Angeles librarian Dan Strehl visited our radio show *Good Food,* he brought along this fabulous recipe for *Manchamanteles,* the first documented California rancho recipe. It is a fascinating amalgamation of sweet roasted fruits and spices, rich meat, and smoky dried chiles. Serve with plain white rice to soak up the savory juices.

2 quarts chicken or beef stock
  or water

2 onions, quartered

1 pound carrots, peeled and
  cut into chunks

2 heads garlic, separated into
  cloves and peeled

4 sprigs thyme, leaves only

2 teaspoons coarse salt, or
  to taste

2¹/₂ pounds boneless pork
  butt, cut into large chunks

3 whole bone-in chicken
  breasts, cut into quarters

Stew

2 large yams (unpeeled), cut
  into 1-inch chunks

1 small pineapple, peeled and
  cut into 1-inch chunks

3 ripe plantains, cut into
  1-inch slices

3 apples, peeled, cored, and
  cut into chunks

2 tablespoons olive oil, plus
  extra for drizzling

coarse salt and freshly ground
  black pepper

Combine the stock, onions, carrots, garlic, thyme, salt, and pork in a large stockpot. Bring to a boil, reduce to a simmer, and cook 1 hour, or until the meat is nearly tender. Add the chicken and simmer 25 to 30 minutes longer, until done. Set aside to cool.

Meanwhile, preheat the oven to 350°F.

To make the stew, place the yams, pineapple, plantains, and apples in a large roasting pan. Drizzle with olive oil, sprinkle with salt and pepper, and toss to coat evenly. Bake 1 hour, stirring occasionally. Set aside to cool.

Wipe the anchos clean and remove the stems, veins, and seeds. Soak in hot water 25 minutes, or until softened, then drain, reserving the liquid. Transfer the chiles to a blender and add the pine nuts, garlic, tomatoes, cumin, oregano, cinnamon, cloves, 2 teaspoons salt, 1 teaspoon pepper, and the brown sugar. Puree until a paste is formed, adding the reserved soaking liquid as needed to thin.

With a slotted spoon, remove the meats and vegetables from broth. Reserve the broth. Thinly slice the meat, and pull the chicken meat from the bones if desired. Arrange the meat, chicken, and vegetables in a large ovenproof casserole.

8 to 10 ancho chiles

$^1/_2$ cup pine nuts

10 garlic cloves, peeled

1 pound ripe tomatoes, cored
and sliced

1 teaspoon ground cumin

1 tablespoon dried oregano,
crumbled

$^1/_4$ teaspoon ground cinnamon

2 whole cloves

2 tablespoons brown sugar

2 tablespoons olive oil

24 pitted prunes

Heat the 2 tablespoons olive oil in a large saucepan over medium-high heat. Pour in the ancho chile paste and cook, stirring occasionally, about 5 minutes, until it thickens. Pour in the reserved broth from the meats and simmer until slightly thickened, 15 to 20 minutes.

Pour the sauce over the meats in the casserole. Add the roasted vegetables and fruits, along with the prunes, and distribute them evenly. Bake about 30 minutes, until bubbly. Serve hot.

Serves 8 to 12

peruvian
lamb stew

Marinade

8 large garlic cloves, peeled

2 tablespoons ground cumin

2 teaspoons coarse salt

2 teaspoons freshly ground
black pepper

$\frac{1}{2}$ cup red wine vinegar

$\frac{1}{4}$ cup olive oil

1 (6-pound) boneless lamb
shoulder, trimmed and cut
into $2\frac{1}{2}$-inch chunks

3 tablespoons olive oil

3 medium onions, chopped

2 teaspoons coarse salt

1 teaspoon freshly ground
black pepper

6 garlic cloves, minced

6 jalapeño chiles, stemmed,
seeded if desired, and
chopped

1 (12-ounce) bottle beer

2 quarts beef or chicken
stock, preferably home-
made, or more if needed

6 large boiling potatoes,
peeled and quartered

1 bunch cilantro, leaves only,
chopped

An exceptionally complex sauce results from first marinating the lamb in a vinegary solution and then stirring some of the marinade into the beer-enhanced stewing liquid. Consider beer for sauces where you want a hint of sweet richness, rather than the acidity of wine.

To make the marinade, in a food processor or blender, combine the garlic, cumin, salt, and pepper and process to a paste. Add the vinegar and olive oil and process to combine. Transfer to a large shallow glass or ceramic baking dish. Add the lamb and toss to coat evenly. Marinate at room temperature 2 to 3 hours.

Lift the lamb from the marinade, reserving $\frac{1}{2}$ cup of the marinade. Heat the olive oil in a large heavy pot or a Dutch oven over high heat. In batches, brown the lamb, adding it in a single layer, turning to sear evenly. With a slotted spoon, transfer the lamb to a plate and set aside.

Reduce the heat to medium-high and add the onions, salt, and pepper. Sauté, stirring frequently, about 10 minutes, until the onions are golden. Add the garlic and jalapeños and cook 2 to 3 minutes longer. Pour in the beer and reduce the heat to medium. Cook about 15 minutes, or until the beer has reduced by half. Stir in the browned lamb, along with its juices and the stock. Bring to a boil, reduce to a simmer, and cook, covered, about 1 hour and 20 minutes, or until the meat is tender.

Add the potatoes, cover, and cook about 20 to 25 minutes more, or until the potatoes are tender. (Add stock or water as needed if the pan is dry.)

Stir in the reserved $\frac{1}{2}$ cup marinade and the cilantro and cook an additional minute. Serve family style at the table.

Serves 6 to 8

sherry-glazed sweetbreads

1 1/2 pounds lamb or veal
   sweetbreads

1 tablespoon freshly squeezed
   lemon juice

1 teaspoon coarse salt

1/2 teaspoon freshly ground
   black pepper

2 tablespoons unsalted butter

2 tablespoons olive oil

Honey-Sherry Vinegar Glaze

1/2 cup finely chopped onion

4 shallots, finely chopped

1/4 cup fino or amontillado
   sherry

2 1/2 tablespoons sherry
   vinegar, or to taste

1 1/2 cups beef or veal stock

1 tablespoon honey

1 tablespoon unsalted butter

Varietal meats do not get the respect they deserve in the American kitchen and we aim to change that one day with an all-offal cookbook! In the meantime, we're content with offering two favorites: this quick sauté of rich, delicious sweetbreads and the Piquant Liver Sauté on page 156.

Soak the sweetbreads in cold water to cover for 2 hours, changing the water a few times.

Drain the sweetbreads and place in a saucepan. Cover with cold water and add the lemon juice. Bring to a boil, reduce to a simmer, and cook 5 minutes. Drain and immediately plunge the sweetbreads into a bowl of ice water for 3 to 4 minutes. Transfer to paper towels to drain.

Separate the sweetbreads into lobes, along the natural divisions, and remove the tubes and connective tissues. The pieces should be approximately 2 inches by 2 inches. Season with the salt and pepper.

In a skillet large enough to hold the sweetbreads in one layer, heat the butter and olive oil over medium heat. Add the sweetbreads and cook about 3 minutes per side, until golden. With a slotted spoon, transfer to a plate and set aside.

To make the glaze, add the onion and shallots to the pan and sauté 5 to 7 minutes, until deep golden. Add the sherry and vinegar, increase the heat to high, and deglaze the pan by stirring and scraping up any browned bits and simmering until the liquid is reduced by half. Pour in the stock and simmer until the liquid is reduced by half, to just under 1 cup. Reduce the heat and whisk in the honey and butter. Return the sweetbreads to the pan, turning to glaze evenly and heat through. Serve immediately.

Serves 4

brazilian marinated steaks with chile lime sauce

4 (1¹/₂-inch thick) shell, sirloin, or rib-eye steaks

¹/₂ cup freshly squeezed lime juice

¹/₃ cup dry red wine

1 small onion, finely chopped

4 garlic cloves, finely chopped

2 teaspoons dried oregano

1 bay leaf

1 teaspoon coarse salt

1 teaspoon freshly ground black pepper

Chile Lime Sauce, recipe follows

Nothing beats a well-marbled rib-eye when the mood strikes for grilled beef. We love to eat steaks with a dab of strong hot chile paste like this rather than a complicated sauce—both components are so direct.

Place the steaks in a single layer in a large glass or ceramic baking dish. Whisk the remaining ingredients together in a bowl and pour over the steaks, turning to coat evenly. Cover and refrigerate 4 to 6 hours, turning occasionally.

Preheat the grill or heat a griddle pan over high heat.

Remove the steaks from the marinade, shaking off the excess, and grill 6 to 8 minutes per side, or until done to taste. Transfer to a platter and let the steaks rest, loosely covered with foil, for 5 minutes, for the juices to settle. Serve with the chile lime sauce.

Serves 4

chile lime sauce

5 to 10 preserved malagueta
   peppers (see Note), chopped

1 teaspoon coarse salt

1 small white onion, finely
   diced

4 large garlic cloves, chopped

juice of 3 limes

$\frac{1}{2}$ bunch Italian parsley,
   leaves only, chopped

Combine all of the ingredients in a mini chopper or a blender, or use a mortar and pestle. Blend or grind until a paste is formed.

Makes about $\frac{1}{2}$ cup

Note: Preserved malagueta peppers are one of the hallmarks of Brazilian cooking. These tiny, extremely hot peppers are pickled in a 2:1 oil to grain alcohol mixture and allowed to sit for 1 month before using. They are available in some Latin American markets, or substitute your favorite pickled hot chiles.

oaxacan
beef stew

3 pounds beef chuck, cut into
    2-inch cubes

1 tablespoon paprika

1 tablespoon ground cumin

coarse salt and freshly ground
    black pepper

flour for dredging

6 tablespoons olive oil

5 medium carrots, peeled and
    quartered lengthwise

1 large chayote (about 1 pound),
    cut into thick slices

6 small red potatoes, quartered

3 medium zucchini, trimmed
    and sliced lengthwise
    $1/4$ inch thick

2 small ripe plantains (about
    $3/4$ pound), sliced diagonally
    $1/2$ inch thick

2 large onions, sliced

2 tablespoons minced garlic

$1^{1}/2$ tablespoons dried Mexican
    oregano, crumbled

2 quarts chicken stock or water

1 cup canned chick peas,
    drained

$1/2$ green cabbage, shredded

$1/4$ pound green beans, trimmed
    and halved

The secret ingredient in this crowd-pleasing stew is the sautéed plantains that permeate and perfume the broth. Feel free to add more root vegetables, such as kohlrabi, parsnips, and rutabaga, along with the carrots for an even sweeter undercurrent of flavor.

Combine the paprika, cumin, 2 teaspoons salt, and 1 teaspoon pepper. Rub the meat all over with the spice mixture. Dredge with flour, shake off the excess, and reserve.

Heat 3 tablespoons of the oil in a large ovenproof casserole over medium-high heat. One at a time, sauté the carrots, chayote, potatoes, zucchini, and plantains until each ingredient is golden, and set aside in a bowl.

Heat the remaining 3 tablespoons oil in the pan until almost smoking, and add the meat. Sear until browned on all sides. Remove with a slotted spoon and set aside.

Add the onions and cook 5 minutes. Add the garlic and oregano and sauté until the garlic's aroma is released. Pour in the chicken stock and return the meat to the pan. Bring to a simmer and cook, covered, about $1^{1}/2$ hours, until the meat is tender.

Add the carrots, chayote, potatoes, zucchini, plantains, and chick peas and simmer 30 minutes.

Stir in the cabbage and green beans. Taste and adjust the seasonings, and cook 20 minutes longer. Serve hot.

Serves 8 to 10

venison scallops with grapefruit and gin

1 large grapefruit

2 1/2 pounds venison loin or
   well-trimmed leg of venison
   (or substitute turkey
   scallops, pounded thin—
   see page 51)

coarse salt and freshly ground
   black pepper

1 1/2 tablespoons olive oil

5 tablespoons cold unsalted
   butter, cut into 10 pieces

10 medium shallots, finely
   diced

1/2 cup gin

6 juniper berries, crushed

1 cup venison or beef stock

1/2 teaspoon cracked black
   pepper, or more to taste

Since venison is being farm-raised these days, it is much less gamey than it used to be and more like a flavorful beefsteak. We like it with juniper berry seasoning, gin, and grapefruit in the sauce. This is delicious with roasted yams and sautéed greens.

Peel the grapefruit and pull it apart into segments. Using the tip of a small sharp knife, loosen the white membrane surrounding each segment and pull it away, trying not to pierce any of the little juice pods. Break up the segments into the juice pods and set aside.

Trim the venison of any tendons or cartilage and cut across the grain into 1/2-inch slices. Place each slice between two sheets of plastic wrap and pound with the flat side of a mallet until just over 1/4 inch thick. Season with salt and pepper.

Preheat the oven to the lowest heat and place a heatproof platter in it.

Heat the olive oil in a large heavy skillet over high heat. Working in batches if necessary, briefly sear the venison scallops, about 1 minute per side. Reduce the heat and cook 1 minute longer, until done to taste—be careful, because venison toughens when cooked beyond medium-rare. Transfer the scallops to the platter and cover loosely with foil.

Wipe the skillet clean and melt 3 tablespoons of the butter over medium heat. Add the shallots and cook 3 to 5 minutes, until caramelized. Add the gin and simmer until reduced by half. Add the juniper berries, stock, 1 teaspoon salt, and the cracked pepper. Increase the heat to high and simmer until the liquid is reduced by one third. Remove from the heat and add the remaining cold butter, whisking until the sauce is smooth and emulsified. Taste for seasoning and stir in the grapefruit.

Place one or two scallops on each plate and spoon the sauce over the top. Serve at once.

Serves 6 to 8

hot tip

KNIFE CARE

Knives should be kept sharp and clean. After cutting anything acidic, immediately wipe the knife clean, since acids can corrode the metal blade. Always wash knives with hot soapy water and towel dry. Do not place in the dishwasher, where blades will get battered. To clean a carbon blade, dip a wine cork in a chlorinated abrasive cleanser such as Ajax and rub off stains. It is best to store knives in a wooden block on the counter or on a magnetic bar on the wall. Avoid kitchen drawers, where they can get damaged banging against other metal tools.

piquant liver sauté

¹/₄ cup sherry vinegar

¹/₄ cup Worcestershire sauce

1 tablespoon dry mustard

4 garlic cloves, mashed to
a paste

1 teaspoon coarse salt

freshly ground black pepper
to taste

8 slices liver, preferably
calves', about ¹/₂ inch thick

8 slices bacon

flour for dusting

2 cups chicken stock

pickled serrano or jalapeño
chiles, for garnish

This quick liver dish comes in a sauce of pan juices enriched with a bit of the marinade and bacon. Sharp pickled chiles are served alongside to offset the richness—instant heaven for liver lovers. Caramelized onions, of course, always make the perfect bed for any liver dish.

Combine the vinegar, Worcestershire, dry mustard, garlic, salt, and pepper in a glass or ceramic baking dish. Add the liver and marinate no longer than 30 minutes.

Fry the bacon in a heavy skillet over medium-high heat until crisp. Transfer the bacon to paper towels to drain, and pour off all but a tablespoon of the bacon fat from the pan.

Lift the liver from the marinade, reserving the marinade. Pat the liver dry and lightly dust with flour.

Place the skillet with bacon fat over high heat and heat until hot. Sear the liver in the pan, about 2 minutes, being careful not to overcook. Transfer the liver to a platter and cover loosely with foil to keep warm.

Drain the fat from the pan. Pour in the reserved marinade and the chicken stock and simmer over medium-high heat until reduced by half. Pour over the liver and serve with the crisp bacon slices and pickled serranos or jalapeños.

Serves 8

RETHINKING THE CENTER OF THE PLATE

We would like to make a case for recasting the American
dinner plate in a way that makes more sense for people and
the planet, and more accurately nourishes modern life. Rather
than focusing on meat or protein as the expensive center of the plate
at our restaurant and at home, we strive for a balance. We may serve
an interesting grain dish, like a toasted rice pilaf, with two or three
freshly cooked vegetables and a salad garnished with leftover meat, for
protein. This way of eating encourages greater variety, which, we are
convinced, is better health-wise. It also is better for the environment
and small farmers, since it keeps more things growing. A couple of
ounces of meat or seafood a day is plenty—except for a couple
of times a year, when we go for that giant rib-eye. When
it comes to the food police, we fall into the Julia
Child camp: Anything and everything is good in
moderation; no food is an outlaw.

sides

In the rush to place the traditional slab of meat on the center of each plate, side dishes tend to get overlooked both in restaurants and at home. Even at upscale restaurants, it is not unusual to find plain, boring side dishes served in skimpy portions—always a depressing sight to us. But at home and at the Border Grill, we treat ourselves well, with flavorful side dishes that bring their distinctive pleasure to the meal. Each of these side dishes has the integrity to stand alone, or, even better, two or three can make an exciting meal—a Susan Feniger blue-plate special. A dish of Swiss Chard with Roasted Garlic matched with rice pilaf would be perfect for a light weeknight dinner with friends. And Mary Sue recommends a weekly roundup of root vegetables for roasting on page 163, an excellent way to use up odds and ends.

papas
anchos

2$\frac{1}{2}$ to 3 pounds boiling
   potatoes (unpeeled),
   quartered

$\frac{1}{4}$ pound feta cheese,
   crumbled

$\frac{1}{4}$ pound añejo cheese, grated

1 teaspoon coarse salt

2 tablespoons olive oil

$\frac{1}{2}$ cup heavy cream or milk

2 ancho chiles, wiped clean,
   stemmed, seeded, and
   julienned

2 scallions, thinly sliced on
   the diagonal

This rustic baked potato casserole develops an extra thread of richness
from strips of dried ancho chiles. Serve with an unfussy chicken dish such
as Red Roasted Chicken (page 100).

Preheat the oven to 350°F.

In a large bowl, combine all of the ingredients except the
scallions and toss well. Transfer to an ovenproof casserole,
cover, and bake 1 hour, or until the potatoes are very tender.
Sprinkle on the scallions and serve.

Serves 6 to 8

mashed roasted eggplant and potatoes

1 medium eggplant

4 large baking potatoes,
  peeled and quartered

$^1/_4$ cup olive oil

$^1/_4$ cup sour cream

1 teaspoon coarse salt

$^1/_2$ teaspoon freshly ground
  black pepper

$^1/_4$ cup grated Cotija or
  añejo cheese

This zingy version of mashed potatoes is the perfect accompaniment to any Mediterranean meal.

Preheat the broiler. Place the eggplant on a baking sheet and roast under the broiler, turning occasionally, until evenly charred and soft all over, 30 to 40 minutes. Transfer to a bowl, along with any juices, and let cool. Then remove the eggplant skin and roughly chop the pulp.

Meanwhile, place the potatoes in a saucepan, generously cover with water, and add salt. Bring to a boil, reduce to a simmer, and cook, uncovered, until soft, 20 to 30 minutes. Drain well and, while they are still warm, mash the potatoes with a potato masher or food mill.

Heat the olive oil in a large skillet over medium heat. Add the chopped eggplant and sour cream and heat through. Fold in the mashed potatoes, mixing well. Season with the salt and pepper, stir in the cheese, and serve immediately.

Serves 6

sweet potato fries

vegetable oil for deep-frying

3 large sweet potatoes, peeled
   and cut lengthwise into
   $1/4$-inch-thick julienne

coarse salt

We've been frying vegetables since we started serving them on our vegetable plate back at City restaurant in the 1980s. Bright-orange sweet potatoes make a terrific chip or fry. For something really special, serve with cracked black pepper and lime juice mayonnaise for dipping.

Pour vegetable oil to a depth of 4 to 5 inches into a large heavy saucepan or deep-fat fryer. Heat to 360°F.

Fry the potatoes, a handful at a time, until cooked through and just lightly colored, 2 to 3 minutes. (The key to consistently good fries is to keep the oil hot. Wait for the oil to reheat between batches.) Remove with a slotted spoon and drain on paper towels. Season with salt and serve hot.

Serves 4 to 6

roasted root vegetables

¹/₂ pound parsnips, peeled and
  cut into 1-inch chunks

¹/₂ pound celery root, peeled
  and cut into 1-inch chunks

¹/₂ pound rutabaga, peeled and
  cut into 1-inch chunks

¹/₂ pound butternut or other
  firm squash, peeled and cut
  into 1-inch chunks

1 onion, coarsely chopped

2 garlic cloves, minced

¹/₂ bunch fresh oregano, leaves
  only, coarsely chopped

¹/₃ cup olive oil

1 teaspoon coarse salt

¹/₂ teaspoon freshly ground
  black pepper

It is hard to go wrong when it comes to roasting root vegetables. Substitute any of your favorites—beets, yams, kohlrabi, turnips, potatoes, carrots, or Jerusalem artichokes—for an almost instant accompaniment to roasted meat or chicken. What a great way to use up overlooked vegetables!

Preheat the oven to 450°F.

In a large bowl, toss together all of the ingredients until well mixed. Arrange in a single layer in an enameled cast-iron casserole or glass baking dish. Cover and roast 30 to 40 minutes, stirring every 10 minutes, until the vegetables are golden, lightly caramelized on the edges, and easily pierced with the tip of a knife. Serve hot.

Serves 6 to 8

mushroom
herb sauté

2 tablespoons olive oil

¹/₂ onion, finely chopped

2 garlic cloves, minced

2 serrano chiles, stemmed,
   seeded, and minced

³/₄ pound oyster mushrooms,
   wiped clean, trimmed, and
   torn into bite-sized pieces

¹/₂ bunch epazote or oregano,
   leaves only, roughly
   chopped

¹/₂ teaspoon coarse salt

¹/₂ teaspoon freshly ground
   black pepper

We were surprised, on our first trip, at how popular mushrooms are in Mexican cooking. The herb epazote is considered mushroom's natural accompaniment much the same way as basil and tomatoes are coupled in the Italian kitchen.

Heat the oil in a large skillet over medium-high heat. Sauté the onion until golden, about 4 minutes. Reduce the heat to low. Add the garlic and chiles and cook 1 minute longer. Add the mushrooms, epazote, salt, and pepper and cook, stirring occasionally, until the mushrooms are wilted and tender, 8 to 10 minutes. Serve immediately.

Serves 4 to 6

swiss chard with roasted garlic

1 ½ pounds Swiss chard, trimmed, washed, and dried

2 tablespoons olive oil

½ small onion, diced

2 serrano chiles, stemmed, seeded, and finely chopped

2 medium tomatoes, cored and finely chopped

10 large cloves Roasted Garlic, page 65, peeled and halved

1 teaspoon coarse salt, or more to taste

Swiss chard, a member of the beet family, is milder and more delicate tasting than the other bitter greens. It is so easy to grow in the California garden and yet it often leaves cooks wondering how to handle it.

In this flavorful dish, we use the whole leaf and cook it just long enough with garlic, tomatoes, and a healthy dose of chiles for an unusual twist. Food this interesting need not be relegated to supporting-player status. Serve with a grain or potato dish for a weeknight vegetarian supper.

Separate the leaves from the stalks of chard. Finely chop the stalks and roughly shred or chiffonade the leaves.

Heat the oil in a large heavy skillet over medium heat. Sauté the onion, chiles, and chard stalks about 1 minute. Add the tomatoes and roasted garlic and cook, stirring, about 3 minutes. Then add the chard leaves and salt. Cover and cook, shaking the pan occasionally, 10 minutes. (Add a few tablespoons of water if the pan seems dry.) Uncover and turn up the heat to high. Cook, stirring occasionally, until the chard is just tender and slightly limp, but not watery, 2 to 4 minutes longer. Adjust the seasoning and serve immediately.

Serves 4 to 6

creamed spinach

2 large bunches spinach,
    stems removed, well washed

1 tablespoon unsalted butter

1 medium onion, finely diced

3/4 cup Crema, page 186, or
    heavy cream

grated nutmeg to taste

1 teaspoon coarse salt

1/2 teaspoon freshly ground
    black pepper

1/4 cup grated añejo cheese

As far as we may travel from the American classics, we will always have a special place in our collective culinary hearts for childhood favorites such as this. We do, however, have a confession to make. It is a myth that spinach is such a supreme source of iron. Apparently the iron in spinach is not wholly assimilable. In any case, it is still a great source of vitamins and minerals and a beautiful, tasty green. We love it creamed and served with simply grilled steak or fish.

Heat a very large deep skillet over medium heat. In two batches, add the spinach, with the water still clinging to its leaves, cover, and cook about 2 minutes. Uncover, toss and stir the leaves, cover, and cook about 2 minutes longer. Remove from the heat and let cool.

With your hands, squeeze the spinach dry, a bunch at a time, removing as much liquid as possible. Coarsely chop and set aside.

Wipe out the skillet, add the butter, and place over medium-low heat. Add the onion and cook, stirring occasionally, until translucent. Pour in the cream, turn up the heat, and simmer until reduced by half. Stir in the spinach, nutmeg, salt, and pepper. Reduce the heat to low and cook just to heat through. Stir in the cheese and serve.

Serves 6

orzo with spinach and pine nuts

3 tablespoons olive oil

2 large bunches spinach,
  stems removed, well washed

coarse salt and freshly ground
  black pepper

$\frac{1}{4}$ cup pine nuts

3 garlic cloves, minced

3 Roma tomatoes, cored,
  seeded, and diced

2 cups orzo pasta

$\frac{1}{4}$ cup grated añejo or
  Romano cheese

Here is another starch-plus-vegetable dish that could easily serve as an entrée for a family meal. It combines lusty Mediterranean flavors with tiny orzo pasta, which is so excellent at absorbing and blending surrounding flavors.

Heat 2 tablespoons of the olive oil in a large skillet over high heat. In two batches, add the spinach, with the water still clinging to its leaves, and stir and toss for 2 minutes, or until the spinach is wilted and tender. Stir in a pinch each of salt and pepper and transfer to a colander set over a bowl to drain.

When the spinach is cool enough to handle, press down to extract as much liquid as possible. Coarsely chop the spinach, reserving the juice.

Wipe out the pan, add the remaining 1 tablespoon olive oil, and place over medium heat. Add the pine nuts and sauté 1 to 2 minutes, until lightly golden. Add the garlic and cook, stirring, about 2 minutes, until its aroma is released. Stir in the tomatoes and the spinach, adjust the seasonings, and cook 1 minute more. Remove from the heat and set aside.

In a large saucepan, bring a generous quantity of lightly salted water to a boil. Cook the orzo, stirring occasionally, about 9 minutes, until tender. Drain thoroughly and transfer to the skillet with the spinach mixture, along with the reserved spinach juice. Toss to mix evenly and taste for seasoning. Reheat gently, sprinkle with the cheese, and serve in pasta bowls.

Serves 6

rice pilaf with corn, chiles, and cheese

1 1/2 tablespoons vegetable oil

1 cup long-grain white rice

1 small onion, finely diced

2 cups hot vegetable or
    chicken stock, preferably
    homemade

3 medium poblano chiles,
    roasted, peeled, seeded,
    and cut into strips

1/2 teaspoon coarse salt

1 cup fresh or thawed frozen
    corn kernels

1/2 cup crumbled Mexican
    queso fresco or feta cheese

1/2 bunch Italian parsley,
    leaves only, finely chopped

Two of our passions are highlighted in this lovely rice dish. We both prefer pilafs to plain white rice and we love the challenge of combining two starches, in this case rice and corn, and coming up with a dish strong enough to be a centerpiece. Try a dinner of this pilaf with Creamed Spinach (page 166) and the Carrot and Currant Salad (page 74).

Heat the oil in a large heavy saucepan over medium heat. Add the rice and onion and cook, stirring frequently, about 7 minutes, until the onion is softened but not browned. Add the hot broth, chiles, and salt, and bring to a boil. Reduce to a simmer and cook, covered, about 10 minutes. Add the corn and simmer 5 minutes longer, or until the rice is tender. Remove from the heat and let stand, covered, about 10 minutes.

Stir in the cheese and parsley, mixing well, and fluff with a fork. Serve immediately.

Serves 6

rice pilaf with chick peas

½ pound dried chick peas, rinsed, picked over, and soaked at least 3 hours, or overnight (or use 3 cups canned chick peas, drained)

2 quarts water

1 bay leaf

3 ounces smoked slab bacon, rind removed, diced

1 large onion, finely chopped

1 yellow bell pepper, cored, seeded, and finely chopped

5 garlic cloves, finely chopped

1½ cups long-grain white rice

¼ cup dry sherry

1½ teaspoons coarse salt

1 teaspoon freshly ground black pepper

Rice gets an extra dollop of richness from chick peas and bacon in this typical Spanish pilaf. Garbanzos, or chick peas, are so popular in Spain that packets of the dried beans are dated for freshness. As a general rule, beans that have been in your pantry longer than a year should be tossed out, since they will be too old and dried out. You know how we feel about combining starches. Yummmm!

Drain the soaked chick peas and combine with the water and bay leaf in a large pot. Bring to a boil, reduce to a simmer, and cook, covered, about 2½ hours, until tender. Drain, reserving the cooking liquid, and discard the bay leaf. There should be 3 cups of liquid—add water if necessary.

Heat a large flameproof casserole over low heat and fry the bacon until lightly browned and just barely crisp. Increase the heat to medium and add the onion. Cook 4 minutes, stirring occasionally. Add the yellow pepper and garlic and cook 4 to 6 minutes more, until all the vegetables are softened.

Tip the pan and spoon off all but about 2 tablespoons of the fat. Add the rice and cook, stirring, about 3 minutes, until well coated and just beginning to brown. Add the sherry, the reserved 3 cups cooking liquid, the chick peas, salt, and pepper. Cook, covered, over medium heat, until most of the liquid has been absorbed and the rice is tender, 25 to 35 minutes. Remove from the heat and let stand 10 minutes, covered.

Fluff the rice with a fork and serve.

Serves 6 to 8

corn and polenta pudding

1 tablespoon unsalted butter, softened

$^1/_2$ cup fine fresh bread crumbs, toasted

1 cup water

$^1/_3$ cup instant polenta

3 cups fresh or thawed frozen corn kernels

1 cup milk

6 large eggs

2 teaspoons sugar

2 teaspoons coarse salt

1 teaspoon freshly ground black pepper

This mild, comforting yellow pudding is especially appealing alongside roasted pork or the stuffed pork chops on page 140.

Preheat the oven to 325°F. Place a heavy baking sheet on the lower rack of the oven. Grease a 2-quart soufflé or shallow baking dish with the butter. Sprinkle with the bread crumbs and shake to evenly coat.

In a small saucepan, bring the water to a boil. Add the polenta, and cook according to the package instructions. (You should have 1 cup of cooked polenta.) Set aside to cool slightly.

In a food processor, combine the corn and milk. Process 10 to 15 seconds, until a rough puree is formed. Transfer to a large bowl and stir in the polenta. Stir in the eggs, one at a time, and then the sugar, salt, and pepper.

Pour into the prepared dish and set on the baking sheet in the oven. Bake until firmly set in the center and beginning to brown around the edges, 50 to 60 minutes. Serve immediately.

Serves 8

hot tip

HOW TO ANCHOR A CUTTING BOARD

To keep the cutting board from wandering while you are chopping, place a damp dish towel under it. Our preference is for wooden cutting boards or, better yet, butcher block counters. We like the way wood breathes and washes clean with soap and water without discoloring. And it's a better surface for cutting, and for our knives, than rigid plastic boards. At home, we protect butcher block counters and cutting boards by rubbing with mineral oil a few times a month.

drunken beans

1 pound dried pinto beans,
rinsed, picked over, and
soaked overnight

3¹/₂ quarts water

¹/₃ cup lard or vegetable oil

2 medium onions, finely
chopped

3 Roma tomatoes, cored,
seeded, and finely chopped

4 serrano chiles, stemmed,
seeded, and finely chopped

1 bunch cilantro, leaves only,
finely chopped

2 teaspoons coarse salt

1 (12-ounce) bottle dark beer

These classic Mexican beans pick up their richness from lard and beer.

Combine the beans and water in a large pot. Cover, bring to a simmer and cook over low heat 1¹/₂ to 2 hours, until the beans are tender. Add more warm water if needed, to prevent scorching. Remove from the heat.

Heat the lard in a large heavy saucepan or skillet over medium-high heat. Sauté the onions until lightly browned. Stir in the tomatoes, chiles, and cilantro and cook for 1 minute. Add the cooked beans, the salt, and beer. Cook, uncovered, over low heat, until the juices have thickened, about 30 minutes. Transfer the hot beans to a decorative clay or ceramic dish and serve.

Serves 8

hot tip

HOW TO STAY COOL

Large pots of soup and beans should be cooled quickly to eliminate the risk of souring. Plunge the pot's bottom into a sink or large bowl of ice water and keep stirring, reaching down to the bottom and turning the beans or other ingredients over, until cool to the touch before refrigerating.

baked sweet
white beans

2 1/4 cups small white or
  cannellini beans, rinsed,
  picked over, and soaked
  overnight

3 cups chicken stock

1/4 cup cider vinegar

1 onion, diced

1 tablespoon grated fresh ginger

1/2 cup packed dark brown sugar

1 tablespoon dry mustard

4 ounces salt pork (or bacon),
  tough outer skin removed
  and cut into 1/2-inch dice

1 teaspoon coarse salt

1/2 teaspoon freshly ground
  black pepper

Salsa

1/2 small red onion, finely diced

1/2 small bunch Italian parsley,
  leaves only, coarsely chopped

2 Roma tomatoes, cored and
  coarsely chopped

2 tablespoons olive oil

2 tablespoons cider vinegar

1 teaspoon soy sauce

1/2 teaspoon coarse salt

1/2 teaspoon freshly ground
  black pepper

We've replaced the pintos with white beans and lightened things with a bright, fresh salsa in this new twist on baked bean casserole. Salt pork is from the same cut of pork as bacon, but it is cured in salt rather than smoked.

Preheat the oven to 300°F.

Drain the soaked beans and rinse with cold running water.

In a medium heavy casserole, combine the chicken stock, vinegar, onion, ginger, brown sugar, and mustard. Whisk together and add the beans and salt pork. Bake, covered, 3 hours, or until the beans have absorbed most of the liquid and the remaining sauce is thick. Stir occasionally to keep the beans evenly moistened and add water as necessary.

About 1 hour before the beans are done, season them with the salt and pepper, and prepare the salsa. Combine all of the salsa ingredients in a small bowl and toss well. Set aside at room temperature.

To serve, ladle the beans into bowls and garnish each with a spoonful of salsa.

Serves 6

desserts

After the fire and heat of Latin foods, we like to linger over a nice, cool ice cream or a simple custard—nothing too fussy or sweet. Interestingly, the cuisines that specialize in the hottest foods—places like India and Mexico— seem to overlook intricate pastries in favor of soothing milk-based dishes, a known antidote to chile's spice. ■ Standouts in this chapter are the Fried Milk, for its shock value—and excellent flavor; Hazelnut Custard Cups, for their pure nutty flavor—minus the crunch; Buttermilk Chocolate Cake, because chocolate is chocolate and everyone needs a great chocolate cake once in a while (especially Susan); and the Honey-Soaked Cookies, for their delightful ability to dissolve on the tongue.

fried
milk

1/2 cup cornstarch

1/2 cup sugar

3 cups milk

2 vanilla beans

2 large eggs

flour for dusting

1 cup fine dry bread crumbs

1/4 cup unsalted butter

3/4 teaspoon ground cinnamon
   mixed with 3 tablespoons
   sugar, for sprinkling

Though many of the traditional Mexican desserts seem pretty weird, even to us, this unusual fried custard is just a delight. We love the contrast of its smooth milky custard against the crisp caramelized crust. It tastes best served right from the sauté pan.

Mix together the cornstarch and sugar in a medium bowl. Whisk in 1 cup of the milk and continue whisking until the cornstarch is completely dissolved. Whisk in the remaining 2 cups milk. Split the vanilla beans lengthwise and scrape the little seeds into the mixture, then add the vanilla beans. Transfer to a medium saucepan.

Place the saucepan over medium heat and bring to a boil, stirring constantly. Continue stirring until the mixture is quite thick, 1 to 2 minutes. Remove the vanilla beans and pour into a shallow glass baking dish, about 8 inches square. Smooth the top with a spatula. Let cool, then cover and refrigerate at least 4 hours, or until quite firm.

Beat the eggs in a shallow bowl. Spread the flour on one plate, and the bread crumbs on another one.

Unmold the custard onto a cutting board. With a sharp knife, cut into approximately 2-inch squares. Dip the squares first into the flour, shaking off the excess, then dip into the beaten eggs and the bread crumbs. Set the squares on a sheet of waxed or parchment paper.

Heat the butter in a heavy 12-inch skillet over medium heat. When the foam begins to subside, add half of the custard squares and brown about 2 minutes on each side, carefully turning with a spatula. Transfer to a platter and finish cooking the squares. Sprinkle with the cinnamon sugar and serve.

Serves 6

hazelnut custard cups

4 ounces hazelnuts, toasted
and skins removed

2¹/₂ cups heavy cream

¹/₂ cup sugar

1 large egg

4 large egg yolks

2 tablespoons Frangelico

a small chunk of semisweet
chocolate, for shaving

hot tip

HOW TO PEEL HAZELNUTS

If you are not finicky about some skins remaining on hazelnuts, just toast and then rub them in a thick terry towel to remove most of the skins. However, if naked is what you want in a hazelnut, here is how to achieve it: Blanch the nuts in a pan of boiling water with two table-spoons baking soda for thirty to forty-five seconds. Drain and rub dry with a towel. Then toast on a baking sheet in a 350°F oven for ten to twelve minutes. The skins will slide right off because the baking soda has neutralized their acidity.

Hazelnuts are such a rich nut that we like to use them like this, so their flavor infuses the custard rather than overwhelming the dish. This great, easy recipe for traditional pots de crème can be adapted to other flavors, with melted chocolate or a coffee infusion.

Grind the hazelnuts in a food processor until fine.

Bring the cream to a boil in a medium saucepan over medium-high heat, being careful not to boil over. Add the sugar and stir until it is dissolved. Stir in the hazelnuts, bring back to a boil, and remove from the heat. Cool nearly to room temperature.

Preheat the oven to 325°F.

In a large bowl, beat together the egg and egg yolks until smooth. Slowly add the cream mixture, stirring constantly. Stir in the Frangelico. Strain the mixture through a fine sieve into a large glass measuring cup with a spout, pressing against the mesh to extract all the flavor from the nuts. Discard the nuts.

Pour the custard mixture into four 6-ounce ramekins and arrange them in a large roasting pan. Pour boiling water into the pan to come halfway up the sides of the custards. Bake on the middle oven rack until the custards are just set in the center, about 35 minutes. Remove from the pan and let cool to room temperature, then chill at least 1 hour.

To serve, use a vegetable peeler to shave chocolate curls, and scatter over each custard.

Serves 4

vanilla flan

Caramel

2 cups sugar

1 ¼ cups water

Flan

6 large eggs

6 egg yolks

½ cup sugar

2 cups half-and-half

2 teaspoons vanilla extract

Homemade Condensed Milk, recipe follows

1 vanilla bean

Mary Sue has been chasing the perfect flan since she first started cooking professionally. This represents her view of perfection (so far)—a supreme flan with a double vanilla kick from both extract and bean. The points to keep in mind when making any flan are: Undercook rather than overcook, bake in a water bath, and test for doneness by looking for a slight shimmer rather than big waves when you press the center. (Beware of air bubbles in the finished product—they are a sign of overcooking.)

To make the caramel, have ready a 9-inch round cake pan. Combine the sugar and ½ cup of the water in a medium saucepan. Use a pastry brush dipped in cold water to wash sugar crystals from the sides of the pan. Cook over medium heat, swirling the pan occasionally, until the mixture is dark brown and has the aroma of caramel, 10 to 15 minutes. Pour enough of the caramel into the cake pan to coat the bottom and sides and swirl to coat evenly. Reserve.

Carefully add the remaining ¾ cup water to the caramel in the saucepan. Bring to a boil and cook over medium heat until the caramel dissolves, about 5 minutes. Stir occasionally and brush down the sides of the pan with a pastry brush dipped in cold water to prevent crystallization. Let cool to room temperature, then chill until serving time.

To make the flan, preheat the oven to 325°F.

In a large bowl, gently whisk together the eggs, egg yolks, sugar, half-and-half, and vanilla extract, without incorporating air.

Pour the condensed milk into a saucepan. Split the vanilla bean lengthwise and, using the tip of a paring knife, scrape the black seeds into the milk. Add the bean and bring to a boil.

Gradually pour the hot milk into the egg mixture, whisking constantly. Pass through a strainer into the caramel-coated cake pan. Place inside a large roasting pan and pour in boiling water to come halfway up the sides of the cake pan.

Bake 1 hour to 1 hour and 10 minutes, until the center feels just set when pressed with your fringertips. Let cool in the water bath. Then remove from the water bath, cover with plastic wrap, and chill at least 6 hours, or overnight.

To serve, run a knife along the inside edge of the pan and gently press the center of the bottom to loosen the flan. Cover with a platter, invert, and remove the pan. Any excess caramel in the pan can be added to the caramel sauce. Cut into wedges to serve, and pass the sauce at the table.

Serves 8 to 10

homemade condensed milk

6 cups nonfat milk

5 tablespoons sugar

Pour the milk into a medium heavy saucepan and bring to a boil. Reduce to a simmer and cook 45 minutes, stirring occasionally. Stir in the sugar and continue simmering until reduced to 3 cups, 10 to 15 minutes. Strain into a container and refrigerate. The milk keeps as long as a week.

Makes 3 cups

crêpes cajeta

1 (14-ounce) can sweetened condensed milk

1 cup milk

1 large egg

2 large egg yolks

1 cup all-purpose flour

2 teaspoons granulated sugar

2 tablespoons unsalted butter, melted

1/2 teaspoon vanilla extract

pinch of ground cloves

pinch of ground cinnamon

1/4 teaspoon salt

1 cup coarsely chopped pecans, toasted

confectioners' sugar, for sprinkling

1 pint fresh raspberries

Cajeta, a caramel sauce used in traditional Mexican desserts, is a terrific dessert sauce to have in your repertoire for instant ice cream sundaes. Think of the method for making cajeta as a slow, steady science experiment whose end result is an excellent and easy sauce.

To make the cajeta, place the unopened can of milk in a heavy saucepan and cover completely with water. Over very low heat, bring the water to a bare quiver and simmer very gently 3 hours, adding more water as necessary to keep the can covered. Wearing an oven mitt, turn the can over and cook for 2 1/2 hours more. Cool to room temperature and refrigerate overnight.

To make the crêpes, in a blender, combine the milk, egg, egg yolks, flour, granulated sugar, butter, vanilla, cloves, cinnamon, and salt. Blend until smooth. Chill 1 hour.

Heat a small nonstick skillet or omelet pan over medium-high heat. Pour in about 2 to 3 tablespoons of the batter, swirling the pan to coat evenly. Cook until small bubbles form on the surface, then flip and cook on the second side until golden. Slide onto a plate and make the remaining crêpes in the same way, stacking them on the plate as you go.

To serve, preheat the oven to 250°F. Open the can of cooked condensed milk and stir well with a fork, blending to an even, thick consistency. Spread about 1 tablespoon of the cajeta evenly over the surface of 1 crêpe. Scatter some of the toasted pecans over the top and roll into a cylinder. Repeat with the remaining crêpes, and reheat in the oven for a few minutes. Arrange 4 crêpes on each plate. Sprinkle with confectioners' sugar, scatter the raspberries over the top, and serve.

Makes about 16 crêpes; serves 4

sweet
tamales

1 (8-ounce) package dried
    corn husks

$1/3$ cup dark raisins or currants

$1/3$ cup chopped dried figs

$1/2$ cup apple juice

$1/2$ cup lard or butter, softened

$3/4$ cup sugar

1 pound ground masa for
    tamales

$1/2$ cup milk, at room
    temperature

1 teaspoon baking powder

$1/4$ teaspoon ground cinnamon

$1/4$ teaspoon salt

Crema, page 186, for serving
    (optional)

1 mango or papaya, peeled,
    seeded, and coarsely
    chopped, for serving
    (optional)

Mary Sue likes to take these sweet, fruity dessert tamales to winter holiday potlucks. They travel easily and can be reheated in a steamer at the party, where they are sure to charm anyone who takes a bite.

Place the husks in a saucepan with water to cover and simmer about 10 minutes. Remove from the heat, weight with a plate to keep the husks submerged, and soak 1 to 2 hours, or overnight, until completely flexible.

Place the raisins and figs in a small pan, cover with the apple juice, and bring to a simmer. Remove from the heat and set aside.

With an electric mixer, beat the lard until light and fluffy, about 1 minute. Add the sugar and half of the masa and beat well to combine. Alternately add the milk and the remaining masa, a bit at a time, beating after each addition, and continue beating until the mixture is the consistency of a thick batter. Beat in the baking powder, cinnamon, and salt and beat 1 minute longer.

Lay 12 of the largest and most flexible husks on a counter, or overlap 2 or 3 smaller ones as necessary for a nice wide surface for each tamale. Make ties for the tamales by cutting a few of the remaining husks into strips. Pat the husks dry with a kitchen towel.

Spread about $1/3$ cup of the batter in the center of each husk. Drain the raisins and figs and scatter over the masa. Fold over the sides and then the ends of each husk to enclose the filling and tie closed with the husk strips.

Line a steamer or a rack fitted into a large pot with corn husks and add the tamales. Steam over simmering water about $2\frac{1}{2}$ hours, or until the husks pull away from the filling easily. Let cool slightly, then unwrap and serve with crema and chopped papaya or mango if desired.

Makes 12 tamales; serves 6

baked apples

1 cup plus 2 tablespoons
   apple juice

$^1/_4$ cup currants

$^1/_4$ cup apricot jam

$^1/_4$ cup chopped toasted
   almonds

2 tablespoons light brown
   sugar

6 medium apples, cored,
   leaving the bottom intact,
   and the top third peeled

2 tablespoons unsalted butter

Crema, page 186, for serving
   (optional)

Susan, who loves a great cheese, recommends serving these delightful baked apples with a platter of Spanish Cabrales, a nutty-flavored blue cheese, and some crema. The best apples for baking are Rome Beauty, Northern Spy, or Winesap.

In a small saucepan, bring 2 tablespoons of the apple juice and the currants to a simmer. Remove from heat and let sit for 10 minutes to plump.

Preheat the oven to 350°F.

In a small bowl, stir together the apricot jam, almonds, and brown sugar. Add the currants with their juice and mix well. Stuff the apples with the jam mixture. Place the apples in a small roasting pan and top each with a dab of the butter. Pour the remaining 1 cup apple juice into the pan and bake 50 to 60 minutes, or until the apples are tender but not split or mushy. Serve hot, with a dollop of crema if desired.

Serves 6

flaming butter-rum plantains

$^1/_2$ cup (1 stick) plus 2 tablespoons unsalted butter

3 large ripe plantains or
   bananas, sliced 1 inch thick
   on the diagonal

$^3/_4$ cup packed dark brown
   sugar

3 tablespoons heavy cream

2 tablespoons dark rum

vanilla ice cream, for serving

Who can resist a flaming dessert? Certainly not Mary Sue. She served her first when she was thirteen, at her aunt and uncle's anniversary dinner. She advises tilting the pan away from you, so the flames go away from your face, and dimming the lights for maximum drama.

In a large heavy skillet, melt ¼ cup of the butter over medium heat. In two batches, add the plantains, in a single layer, and fry until golden, about 4 minutes per side. With a slotted spoon, remove to a plate, and cover with foil to keep warm.

Add the brown sugar, the remaining 6 tablespoons butter, and the cream to the pan and stir over medium heat until the sugar has dissolved. Then increase the heat to high and bring to a boil. Cook 2 minutes, until slightly thickened. Return the plantains to the pan and stir to coat evenly. Pour in the rum, remove from the heat, and immediately light with a match. Spoon the flaming plantains over bowls of vanilla ice cream and serve.

Serves 6

hot tip
DON'T TOSS THOSE BUTTER WRAPPERS!
Susan is obsessed with saving the papers that butter comes wrapped in. She likes to keep them folded in a plastic Ziploc bag in the refrigerator for use whenever buttered parchment is called for or as an excellent seal when reheating cooked foods such as rice. Just place one or more over the top and heat without fear of dryness.

pear and golden raisin crisp

³/₄ cup sugar

2 tablespoons tapioca

6 medium ripe pears (about 3 pounds), thinly sliced

juice of ¹/₂ lemon

¹/₂ cup golden raisins

¹/₂ cup dark rum

Topping

¹/₂ cup packed light brown sugar

¹/₄ cup unsalted butter, cut into ¹/₂-inch cubes

1 cup all-purpose flour

³/₄ cup sliced unblanched almonds

¹/₂ teaspoon ground cinnamon

¹/₄ teaspoon salt

Crema, recipe follows, or ice cream, for serving (optional)

We devoted an entire show to pears, the most neglected winter fruit, and one of Mary Sue's favorites. This classic American crisp with its crumbly brown sugar topping is terrific after a casual supper or brunch. Crisps are also delightful reheated for breakfast and served with a dollop of plain yogurt or cream.

In a large bowl, combine the sugar and tapioca and toss to mix. Add the pears and lemon juice and toss until evenly coated. Let stand 30 minutes, or until the juices are released and the tapioca softens.

Meanwhile, in a small bowl, combine the raisins and rum in a small saucepan and bring to a boil. Remove from the heat and set aside to plump and cool.

Preheat the oven to 350°F.

To make the topping, in a large bowl, beat the brown sugar and butter until creamy. Add the flour, almonds, cinnamon, and salt and gently mix until crumbly.

Stir the raisins and rum into the pear mixture. Spoon into a 10-inch round baking dish, preferably glass. Sprinkle the crumb mixture evenly over the top and bake about 40 minutes, until the topping is golden. Cool on a rack 10 minutes and serve warm, with a dollop of cream or ice cream if desired.

Serves 8

crema

2 cups heavy cream

¼ cup buttermilk

Whisk the cream and buttermilk together in a bowl. Cover and set in a warm place (a gas oven with just the heat from the pilot light is fine) for 8 hours or until thickened. Crema may be kept in the refrigerator as long as a week.

Makes 2 cups

hot tip

ON BUTTER

We always use unsalted butter for cooking and baking because it is usually fresher (since salt is a preservative, salted butter can stay on the grocery shelf longer) and it allows us to control the amount of salt in the finished dish.

buttermilk chocolate cake with coconut-pecan marmalade

3 ounces unsweetened
   chocolate, coarsely
   chopped

$1/2$ cup (1 stick) unsalted
   butter, softened

$1^{1}/2$ cups sugar

2 large eggs

1 teaspoon vanilla extract

$1/2$ teaspoon salt

2 cups all-purpose flour

1 cup buttermilk

1 teaspoon baking soda

1 tablespoon cider vinegar

Coconut Pecan Marmalade
   (page 190)

A truly great chocolate birthday cake must be one of the keys to a happy childhood. With this recipe, similar to a German chocolate cake but with buttermilk and unsweetened chocolate for added acidity, you (and your children) will never be disappointed come birthday time. We promise.

Preheat the oven to 350°F. Butter a 9-inch round cake pan and line the bottom with parchment paper. Butter the paper.

In a double boiler or a heatproof bowl over a small pot, melt the chocolate over simmering water, stirring occasionally. Set aside to cool slightly.

With an electric mixer, in a large bowl, cream the butter and sugar until light and fluffy. Add the eggs one at a time, beating for 2 minutes after each addition. Beat in the vanilla and salt. Beat in the melted chocolate.

Add the flour and buttermilk alternately, in three batches, mixing well after each addition. Stir together the baking soda and vinegar and add to the batter, stirring just until combined.

Pour into the prepared cake pan, smoothing the top. Bake 35 to 45 minutes, or until a toothpick inserted in the center comes out clean. Cool in the pan 5 minutes, then turn out onto a rack to finish cooling.

With a serrated knife, slice the cake into three layers. With a soft pastry brush, brush any loose crumbs from the edges.

To assemble the cake, place a layer on a serving dish. Spread a $1/2$-inch-thick layer of coconut marmalade over the top. Top with a second layer and spread with an even layer of marmalade. Place the third cake layer on top and spread a thick layer of the remaining marmalade over the top and sides, mounding it slightly on top.

Serves 6 to 8

hot tip

ON FRESH GINGER

We like to find the sweet, spicy
kick of freshly grated ginger in
unexpected places, such as seared
greens, salsas, and stews. When shopping, look for firm pieces with smooth,
unwrinkled skins and no mold. They
should feel solid and reverberate when
knocked against a counter. Peel ginger
with a knife and rub against a ceramic
ginger grater or mince in a food
processor with a bit of rice vinegar.
Since ginger loses its freshness
fast, just chop what you need
and store the leftover piece
in the freezer.

pumpkin cheesecake tarts with gingersnap crust

Crust

4 cups finely crushed
   gingersnaps (about 60)

$^1/_2$ cup (1 stick) unsalted
   butter, melted

Filling

1 tablespoon grated fresh
   ginger

1 pound cream cheese,
   softened

$^1/_2$ cup packed light brown
   sugar

$^1/_2$ teaspoon ground cinnamon

pinch of grated nutmeg

pinch of ground allspice

pinch of ground cloves

$^1/_4$ teaspoon salt

$^3/_4$ cup fresh or canned
   pumpkin puree

2 large eggs

These tartlets have all the sweet winter spices we love, a luscious creamy interior, and extra snap in the ginger cookie crust. Cheesecakes are so popular and so easy to make that they are a good choice for beginning bakers.

Preheat the oven to 325°F.

To make the crust, in a bowl, combine the gingersnap crumbs with the melted butter and toss together until the mixture holds together when pressed. (Add an additional tablespoon of melted butter if necessary.) Pat evenly over the bottom and halfway up the sides of eight 4$^1/_2$-inch tartlet pans or one 10-inch springform pan. Bake about 7 minutes, or until set. Remove from the oven.

Meanwhile, make the filling. Put the grated ginger in a fine sieve set over a small bowl and press against it to extract the juice. Set aside the ginger juice and discard the pulp.

In the bowl of an electric mixer, combine the cream cheese, brown sugar, cinnamon, nutmeg, allspice, cloves, and salt. Beat until creamy and well combined, then beat in the ginger juice and the pumpkin puree. Add the eggs one at a time, beating after each until blended but being careful not to overbeat. Pour the filling into the tartlet pans or springform pan. Bake 25 to 30 minutes for tartlets, about 40 minutes for cake, or until the center is just firm to the touch. Cool to room temperature, then chill at least 2 hours, or overnight, before serving.

Serves 8

coconut pecan marmalade

1 (12-ounce) can
evaporated milk

1 cup packed light brown
sugar

5 large egg yolks, lightly
beaten

1/2 cup (1 stick) unsalted
butter

1 teaspoon vanilla extract

1 1/2 cups flaked sweetened
coconut

1 1/2 cups pecan pieces,
toasted

Combine the milk, brown sugar, egg yolks, butter, and vanilla in a medium saucepan. Cook, stirring constantly, over medium heat until smooth and thick, about 10 minutes; do not let boil. Remove from the heat and add the coconut and pecans. Stir well and let cool to room temperature, beating occasionally to prevent a crust from forming.

honey-soaked cookies

3/4 cup corn oil

1/3 cup sugar

grated zest of 1 orange

2 tablespoons freshly
   squeezed orange juice

2 to 2 1/4 cups all-purpose flour

3/4 teaspoon baking powder

1/4 teaspoon baking soda

1/4 teaspoon salt

Syrup

1 cup sugar

3/4 cup water

1/2 cup honey

1/2 cup toasted pine nuts,
   chopped

These crumbly, fragrant, light cookies, similar to traditional Greek honey cookies, dissolve on the tongue. They are a little messy—place in individual paper cups for less dripping honey.

Preheat the oven to 325°F. Grease a large baking sheet.

In a large bowl, combine the corn oil, sugar, orange zest, and juice and beat until thoroughly combined.

In a small bowl, combine 1/2 cup of the flour, the baking powder, and baking soda. Add to the corn oil mixture and beat well. Add the remaining flour 1/4 cup at a time, and mix until a medium-stiff dough is formed. The finished dough should hold a shape.

Break off pieces of the dough a tablespoonful at a time and pat into 2-inch-long oval egg-shaped cakes. Arrange 1 1/2 inches apart on the baking sheet. Bake 25 to 30 minutes, until just golden. Cool on wire racks.

To make the syrup, combine the sugar, water, and honey in a small saucepan and bring to a boil. Boil 2 minutes, then reduce to a simmer. With a slotted spoon, gently dip each cooled cookie into the syrup just for a moment, making sure to coat evenly all over. Transfer to wire racks and immediately sprinkle with the pine nuts. Let set on the rack for 30 seconds or so before serving.

Makes 20 to 25 cookies

almond surprise cookies

3/4 cup (1 1/2 sticks) unsalted butter, softened

1 cup sugar

1 large egg

1 tablespoon vanilla extract

1/2 teaspoon almond extract

2 cups sifted all-purpose flour

1/2 teaspoon salt

1/2 cup coarsely chopped almonds

1/4 cup whole unblanched almonds

1/4 cup unsweetened cocoa powder

1/4 cup confectioners' sugar

To hide a whole almond in the center of a cookie is a typical Latin trick. These are easy treats for holiday cookie platters.

Preheat the oven to 350°F.

In a large bowl, cream the butter and sugar until fluffy. Beat in the egg, vanilla, and almond extract. Sift the flour over the top, add the salt and chopped almonds, and mix to combine thoroughly.

Break off generous teaspoonfuls of dough and roll between your palms into 1-inch balls. Press an almond into the center of each, enclosing it completely with dough. Place 1 inch apart on ungreased baking sheets and bake 15 to 20 minutes, until lightly browned. Transfer to racks to cool slightly.

When cool enough to handle, roll half of the cookies in the cocoa powder and the remaining half in the confectioners' sugar to coat. Return to the rack to cool completely.

Makes about 28 cookies

guava pastry diamonds

2 ¼ cups sifted all-purpose flour

¾ cup (1 ½ sticks) unsalted butter, cut into ½-inch pieces

1 teaspoon sugar

¼ teaspoon salt

6 tablespoons Crema, page 186, or crème fraîche

¼ teaspoon vanilla extract

4 ounces guava paste, broken up

1 ½ teaspoons freshly squeezed lemon juice

1 egg, lightly beaten

Guava is often used in Mexican breakfast pastries. We like its slightly sour, rich flavor and distinctive aroma in these delicate miniature pastries, adapted from a recipe we learned back in Chicago at one of our first restaurant jobs.

In a large bowl, combine the flour, butter, sugar, and salt. With your fingertips, rub the mixture together, until pea-sized crumbs form. Add the crema and vanilla and mix together just until the dough comes together. Gather the dough into a ball and flatten it into a disk. Wrap with plastic wrap and refrigerate at least 2 hours.

Preheat the oven to 400°F. Lightly oil a baking sheet.

In a food processor or blender, pulse the guava paste with the lemon juice until a smooth paste forms.

On a lightly floured surface, roll out the pastry to a ¼-inch-thick rectangle. With a sharp blade, cut into 4-inch squares. Place a small spoonful of the guava paste in the center of each square. Dab a little beaten egg on the inside of one corner and the outside of the opposite corner. Bring the two edges together, overlapping them and covering most of the paste, and press together lightly to seal.

Transfer the squares to the baking sheet and bake about 25 minutes, or until lightly golden. Cool on a rack and serve warm or at room temperature.

Makes 12 to 14 diamonds

coffee brownies

5 ounces unsweetened chocolate, coarsely chopped

1 ¼ cups (2 ½ sticks) unsalted butter, softened

¼ cup finely ground espresso beans

½ teaspoon salt

2 ½ cups sugar

5 large eggs

1 teaspoon vanilla extract

1 ¼ cups all-purpose flour

1 cup pecans, coarsely chopped

Glaze

¼ cup Kahlúa

1 teaspoon vanilla

1 tablespoon softened butter

1 cup powdered sugar

Since we opened our first restaurant, brownies have always found a place on the menu—they are so easy to make and so universally loved. For cocktail parties, try cutting brownies into tiny bite-sized squares so everyone can leave the party happy, having had their sweet chocolate ending. Brownies freeze so well that we often keep a tray in the restaurant freezer for emergencies.

Preheat the oven to 325°F. Butter and flour a 9 × 12-inch baking pan and line the bottom with parchment paper. Butter and flour the paper.

Combine the chocolate, butter, espresso, and salt in the top of a double boiler or a heatproof bowl set over simmering water. Heat, stirring, until melted and smooth. Let cool.

In a large bowl, combine the sugar, eggs, and vanilla and whisk until smooth. Add the melted chocolate mixture and whisk until well combined. Fold in the flour just until it disappears. Gently fold in the pecans. Pour into the prepared pan, smoothing the top.

Bake about 35 minutes, or until a toothpick inserted in the center comes out clean.

For the glaze, whisk together the Kahlúa, vanilla, and butter until incorporated. Add the powdered sugar and beat until a smooth icing forms. Spread over the cooled brownies and let set 1 hour or more before cutting into squares. Lift out and transfer to a serving plate or a tin.

Makes 12 large or 20 small brownies

champagne jelly with raspberries

2 (¹/₂-ounce) packets
  unflavored gelatin

1¹/₂ cups water

1 cup sugar

zest of 1 lemon, removed
  in strips

juice of 1 lemon

2 cups Champagne, dry
  sherry, or dry white wine

1 cup fresh raspberries

6 small mint sprigs, for
  garnish

Champagne-flavored gelatin may sound strange, but this dish is one of the most perfect endings to a big, heavy meal that we know. A dish that juxtaposes a familiar flavor with an unexpected texture is always provocative. It would also be delicious with a fino sherry.

In a small bowl, soften the gelatin in 3 tablespoons of the water.

In a saucepan, heat the remaining 1¹/₄ cups plus 1 tablespoon water over low heat and add the gelatin. Stir until the gelatin dissolves. Add the sugar, lemon zest, and juice. Bring to just below a boil and remove from the heat. Cover and let steep 20 minutes.

Strain the gelatin mixture through a fine sieve into a shallow bowl. Set aside to cool 10 to 15 minutes.

When the gelatin is cool to the touch, stir in the Champagne. Pour into tall Champagne flutes and drop a few raspberries into each. Chill until set.

Serve garnished with the remaining raspberries and the sprigs of mint.

Serves 6

hot tip

HOW TO REMOVE A STUBBORN CAKE
When cakes and brownies cool in the pan, sometimes the butter solidifies on the bottom, forming a seal. To loosen, briefly warm the bottom of the pan over a low flame, then invert and remove.

pink grapefruit sorbet

3 cups freshly squeezed pink
   grapefruit juice (reserve
   2 grapefruit halves for
   serving)

3/4 cup simple syrup
   (See Note)

3 tablespoons white tequila

1/2 pint ripe strawberries,
   hulled and sliced

The idea for serving sorbet in hollowed-out grapefruit halves comes from the Mexican habit of emptying limes for use as tequila shot glasses. Though that makes a nice presentation for a party, the sorbet is equally delicious served in simple glass dessert cups.

In a bowl, mix the pink grapefruit juice with the simple syrup and tequila. Pour into an ice cream machine and freeze according to the manufacturer's directions. Transfer to a container and freeze until serving time. Wrap and freeze the reserved grapefruit halves.

Place the sorbet in the refrigerator for 15 minutes before serving to soften slightly.

Scatter half the strawberry slices over the bottom of the frozen grapefruit halves. Scoop the sorbet over the strawberries, and cover with the remaining berries.

Makes 4 cups

Note: To make simple syrup, combine 1/2 cup sugar and 1/3 cup water in a small saucepan and bring to a boil. Boil until the sugar dissolves and the syrup is clear. Let cool and refrigerate until needed; the syrup keeps, refrigerated, 2 weeks or more.

frozen banana custard

2 cups milk

4 large eggs

1 cup packed dark brown
   sugar

1 teaspoon vanilla extract

3 large ripe bananas, peeled

juice of 1 lemon

Ruth's Hot Fudge Sauce,
   recipe follows, for serving

chopped, toasted peanuts,
   for serving

Never judge a dessert by its cover. When we designed this easy custard, we had in mind a rich homemade milk dessert for people who don't own an ice cream maker. So while the tastes are fabulous, its appearance may leave something to be desired—brown is the dominant color. Still, when you serve it coated with hot fudge sauce and dotted with peanuts, we guarantee you won't hear any complaints.

In a medium saucepan, bring the milk just to a boil. Remove from the heat and let cool slightly.

In a medium bowl, stir together the eggs, brown sugar, and vanilla. Stir about ½ cup of the warm milk into the egg mixture. Then pour the egg mixture into the pan with the milk. Cook over medium-low heat, stirring constantly, until the mixture thickens and coats the back of a spoon; do not boil. Remove from the heat.

Place the bananas in a food processor and pulse to a smooth puree. Add the warm custard mixture and pulse 2 or 3 times, scraping down the sides of the bowl, until evenly blended. Let cool to room temperature, then transfer to a shallow metal pan. Freeze at least 6 hours, or overnight.

Let the custard soften 5 to 10 minutes before serving. Scoop into bowls and top with the hot fudge sauce and peanuts.

Serves 6

ruth's hot fudge sauce

8 ounces unsweetened
   chocolate, chopped

2 cups sugar

3 tablespoons double-strength
   coffee

2 tablespoons vanilla extract

pinch of salt

1 $^1/_3$ to 1 $^1/_2$ cups evaporated
   milk

Melt the chocolate in a double boiler or a bowl set over simmering water. Add the sugar and stir to combine. Cover and cook over hot water for 30 minutes.

Add the coffee, vanilla, and salt. Stir to combine. Then gradually add the evaporated milk, stirring until smooth and glossy. Remove from the heat.

Serve over frozen custard or ice cream. Fudge sauce keeps in the refrigerator for several weeks. To reheat, warm in the microwave 1 minute at full power or on the stovetop over low heat.

Makes 1 $^1/_2$ cups

orange
ice cream

7 oranges, well scrubbed

²/₃ cup freshly squeezed
    lemon juice

8 large egg yolks

1 ¹/₃ cups sugar

2 cups heavy cream

1 cup half-and-half

¹/₄ cup nonfat dry milk powder

2 teaspoons vanilla extract

Since you can't buy really great orange ice cream, we decided to make our own, reminiscent of our City restaurant lemon ice cream and delicious in its own right. A scoop of this unusually intense ice cream is perfect all alone, but with a butter cookie or the Honey-Soaked Cookies (page 191), it makes a sensational dessert.

Grate the zest of all the oranges, taking care not to include any of the white pith. Squeeze 2 cups of the juice. Combine the orange juice with the lemon juice in a bowl and set aside.

In a large bowl, combine the egg yolks and sugar and whisk until pale yellow and thick.

In a medium heavy saucepan, combine the cream, half-and-half, nonfat dry milk, and orange zest and bring to a boil over medium-high heat. Remove from the heat and pour into the yolk mixture, whisking constantly until well combined. Stir in the citrus juices and the vanilla. Strain into a large container and chill until cold.

Freeze in an ice cream maker according to the manufacturer's instructions. Store in the freezer.

Makes 1¹/₂ quarts

horchata ice cream with cinnamon and pecans

1 quart nonfat milk

1 vanilla bean

4 cinnamon sticks

$^1/_2$ cup rice

$^1/_4$ cup nonfat dry milk

5 large egg yolks

$^1/_2$ cup granulated sugar

$^1/_2$ cup packed brown sugar

2 cups heavy cream

1 $^1/_2$ cups toasted pecan
    halves, roughly chopped

Horchata, the traditional rice drink of Mexico, makes a mysterious base for this creamy, rich, white ice cream dotted with crunchy pecans.

Pour the nonfat milk into a heavy saucepan. Split the vanilla bean lengthwise and, using the tip of a paring knife, scrape the black seeds into the milk. Add the bean and the cinnamon, bring to a simmer, and cook about 15 minutes. Let cool, then strain into a bowl; you should have about 2½ cups liquid.

Combine the rice and nonfat dry milk in a blender. Process until the rice is finely ground, and stir into the milk.

Whisk together the egg yolks and both sugars in a large bowl.

Meanwhile, bring the cream nearly to a boil in a small saucepan. Whisking gently, pour the cream into the egg mixture, then add the reserved milk mixture. Whisk well. Let cool, then chill.

Pour the chilled custard mixture into an ice cream maker and process according to the manufacturer's instructions. Just before the ice cream is frozen, add the toasted pecans. Store in the freezer.

Makes 1½ quarts

hot tip

KITCHEN PLANNING

Keep the utensils you use most often—spatulas, slotted spoons, whisks, and tongs—in a large container on the kitchen counter, preferably close to the stovetop. Cooking becomes much less of a chore when your kitchen is efficiently organized and the tools you need are handy.

brunch

When it comes to serving brunch, the pressure should be off. That is why we designed this chapter with an eye toward unfussy, straightforward foods that don't call for a great deal of last-minute cooking, technical expertise, or unusual ingredients. On the other hand, they all deliver a great deal of flavor and all-around enjoyment. So whether you choose to make tender, homemade Buttermilk Biscuits with spicy jalapeño jam to brighten your late-morning eggs or you aim to impress with a casserole of Baked Eggs with Peppers and Peas, relax and enjoy the weekend by sharing a meal with friends. And don't forget the Café de Olla!

baked eggs with peppers and peas

Sofrito

¹/₄ cup olive oil

¹/₂ onion, finely chopped

2 large garlic cloves, minced

2 red bell peppers, roasted, peeled, and seeded, one finely chopped, the other cut into ¹/₂-inch strips

3 ounces prosciutto, finely diced

2 large tomatoes, cored, seeded, and finely chopped

¹/₂ bunch Italian parsley, leaves only, roughly chopped

2 small bay leaves

1 teaspoon coarse salt

¹/₂ teaspoon freshly ground black pepper

¹/₃ cup water

6 large eggs

³/₄ cup cooked fresh or frozen peas

3 tablespoons dry sherry (optional)

chunks of grilled country bread, for serving

If you like to do a minimum of last-minute cooking when you entertain, make the sofrito for this impressive egg dish early in the morning. Then all you need to do is crack open the eggs, garnish, and bake while you and your guests relax over some spicy Bloody Marys.

Preheat the oven to 400°F.

To make the sofrito, heat the oil a large heavy skillet over medium heat. Sauté the onion 4 to 6 minutes, until lightly golden. Add the garlic and chopped red pepper and cook 2 to 3 minutes more, until the vegetables are softened but not browned. Stir in the prosciutto and cook 2 minutes. Add the tomatoes, parsley, bay leaves, salt, pepper, and water and bring to a simmer. Cook until the mixture is nearly dry. Remove from the heat and discard the bay leaves.

Spread the sofrito evenly in a 9-inch square ceramic or earthenware casserole. One at a time, carefully break the eggs onto the sofrito, forming a circle. Heap the peas in mounds between the eggs, and frame the eggs with the pepper strips. Sprinkle the sherry over the top if desired, and bake 20 minutes, or until the eggs are cooked to taste. Serve immediately, accompanied by chunks of grilled country bread.

Serves 6

roasted chile frittata

12 large eggs, lightly beaten

1 to 2 teaspoons good-quality pure chile powder (page 134)

1 teaspoon coarse salt

$\frac{1}{2}$ teaspoon freshly ground black pepper

$\frac{1}{2}$ bunch cilantro, leaves only, finely chopped, plus cilantro sprigs for garnish

1 tablespoon olive oil

1 small onion, finely chopped

1 $\frac{1}{2}$ red bell peppers, roasted, peeled, seeded, and sliced into strips

2 poblano chiles, roasted, peeled, seeded, and diced

1 cup grated Mexican Manchego or Monterey Jack cheese

Italian frittatas, or omelets, are a great choice for weekend brunch since they can be cooked ahead and served at room temperature. One of our pet peeves is overcooked eggs: Take your time and cook the eggs slowly, then just run them under the broiler very briefly, simply to firm the top, not to brown it too much.

In a large bowl, combine the eggs, chile powder, salt, pepper, and cilantro. Whisk until well blended and set aside.

Heat the olive oil in an ovenproof 10-inch nonstick skillet over medium heat. Sauté the onion 5 to 6 minutes, until softened and lightly golden. Add the red peppers and poblanos and cook 2 minutes more. Pour the egg mixture into the pan, swirling the pan to make an even layer. Reduce the heat to medium-low, scatter the cheese over the top, and cook, covered, until the eggs are nearly set. (Shake the pan occasionally to prevent sticking.)

Meanwhile, preheat the broiler.

Place the pan under the broiler for a minute or two to set the top. Remove from the heat and let cool in the pan for 10 minutes.

Place a round platter on top of the pan and invert to remove the frittata. Serve warm or at room temperature, garnished with cilantro sprigs and cut into wedges.

Serves 6 to 8

corn pancakes with maple fruit compote

2 cups finely ground cornmeal,
   preferably organic

1/2 cup all-purpose flour

2 teaspoons baking soda

1/2 teaspoon coarse salt

1 tablespoon sugar

1/2 cup (1/2 stick) unsalted
   butter

2 cups buttermilk

1/4 to 1/2 cup milk

butter or oil for coating

Maple Fruit Compote,
   recipe follows, for serving

Organic cornmeal, especially that from Arrowhead Mills, has a much sweeter flavor and finer texture than ordinary cornmeal. We made these easy pancakes at the Santa Monica farmers' market and sold out in minutes. For really easy early morning treats, the pancakes can be made in advance and frozen in individual plastic sandwich bags, double-packed in Ziploc bags. To reheat, arrange in a single layer on a baking sheet and warm in a 350°F oven about ten minutes.

Preheat the oven to 250°F.

In a bowl, combine the cornmeal, flour, baking soda, salt, sugar, and butter. Blend together with your fingertips or a pastry blender until the consistency of a coarse meal.

Pour in the buttermilk and stir just until the dry ingredients are evenly moistened. Add just enough milk to form a thin pancake batter, stirring gently to combine.

Heat a griddle or large cast-iron skillet over medium heat and lightly coat with butter or oil. Ladle on about 1/4 cup of the batter and cook until bubbles form on the surface of each pancake and the bottom is golden brown. Flip and cook on the second side until golden, about 1 minute. Transfer to a paper towel–lined baking sheet and keep warm in the oven while you cook the rest of the pancakes. Serve hot, topped with the fruit compote.

Makes 12 large pancakes; serves 4 to 6

maple fruit compote

2 ¹/₂ cups sliced assorted very
ripe stone fruit, such as
peaches, plums, apricots,
and/or cherries

³/₄ cup maple syrup

Combine the fruit and maple syrup in a bowl and serve at room temperature, or cover and refrigerate until an hour before serving.

Makes about 3 cups

potato, chorizo, and egg scramble

2 russet potatoes, peeled and
  diced

$1/2$ pound bulk or finely
  chopped chorizo

1 onion, chopped

coarse salt and freshly ground
  black pepper

10 large eggs, beaten until
  frothy

$1/2$ bunch cilantro, leaves only,
  chopped

3 scallions, sliced

grated panela cheese, for
  garnish (optional)

This hearty meal is a typical spicy Mexican breakfast. Complete the picture with sides of refried beans, mashed avocado, salsa fresca, some nice warm corn tortillas, and pitchers of fresh fruit juice or the Cantaloupe Liquado on page 218.

Cook the potatoes in a large saucepan of boiling salted water until just barely tender, about 10 minutes. Drain and set aside.

In a large nonstick skillet, sauté the chorizo, breaking up any lumps, until browned. Drain off any excess oil. Add the onion and salt and pepper to taste and cook 3 to 5 minutes, until golden. Add the potatoes and cook until well browned, about 10 minutes.

Add the beaten eggs and cook, stirring with a fork to scramble, until softly set but not browned. Just before the eggs set, stir in the cilantro and scallions. Garnish with cheese if desired, and serve.

Serves 4

turkey-cilantro sausages

2 pounds light and dark turkey meat, trimmed and cut into chunks

$1/2$ pound high-quality pork fatback, cut into 1-inch chunks

$1/4$ cup dry white wine

2 jalapeño chiles, stemmed, seeded, and minced

2 teaspoons ground dried chipotle chile or $1/2$ canned chile chipotle en adobo, rinsed and finely chopped

$1/2$ bunch fresh cilantro, leaves only, finely chopped

2 teaspoons coarse salt

1 teaspoon freshly ground black pepper

The trick to making superb sausages is to start with the right proportion of meat to fat and then to keep everything—ingredients, bowl, and grinder—ice-cold. For a delightful sandwich, try serving these patties on Buttermilk Biscuits with Jalapeño Jam (page 214) slathered on with fried eggs on the side.

On a tray covered with plastic wrap, freeze the turkey and fatback for 30 minutes to firm.

In a heavy-duty mixer fitted with the grinder attachment, or in a food processor, grind the meat and fatback together, in short bursts if using a food processor. The mixture should be coarsely ground, not pulverized.

In a large bowl, combine the ground meat and fat, the wine, jalapeño and chipotle chiles, cilantro, salt, and pepper using your hands, mix together until well blended, being careful not to overmix, or the meat will become warm and the fat will melt. Cover and chill 2 hours to allow the flavors to marry.

Form the mixture into 12 flat patties approximately 3 inches in diameter.

Heat a large cast-iron or nonstick pan or griddle over medium-low heat. Fry the sausage patties, in batches, until golden, turning once, about 4 minutes total. Drain excess fat from the pan as necessary. Briefly drain on paper towels and serve hot.

Makes 12 patties

jícama pancakes with apple-tamarind sauce

1 ½ cups shredded peeled
    jícama

juice of 1 lime

½ small onion, grated

½ teaspoon minced seeded
    habanero chile

1 large egg, beaten

2 tablespoons all-purpose
    flour

1 teaspoon coarse salt

1 russet potato, peeled

about ¼ cup vegetable oil

Apple-Tamarind Sauce,
    recipe follows, for serving

Serve these spicy, crunchy pancakes with Turkey-Cilantro Sausages (page 209) for brunch or as a vegetable side for a dinner of brisket or a steak. They are just the kind of simple, surprising food that reawakens tired taste buds.

In a colander, toss the jícama with the lime juice and let sit 15 minutes.

With your hands, squeeze the jícama to release its water. Spread on a double layer of paper towels and pat dry with additional towels.

In a large bowl, combine the jícama with the onion, chile, egg, flour, and salt and mix well. Using the largest holes of a grater, grate the potato into the bowl, and mix again.

Preheat the oven to 250°F.

Heat 1 tablespoon of the oil in a large cast-iron skillet over medium-high heat until very hot. Using two spoons, drop the batter by large spoonfuls into the hot oil. Flatten into 2½-inch patties and cook until brown on the bottom. Flip and cook on the second side until golden brown and crisp. Transfer to a paper towel–lined baking sheet and keep warm in the oven while you finish cooking the pancakes; add more oil to the skillet as needed. Serve warm, with the sauce over one side of the pancakes.

Makes 12 pancakes; serves 4

apple-tamarind sauce

2 ounces tamarind pulp
(available in Latin and
Asian markets)

1 cup boiling water

¹/₄ cup honey

4 cooking apples, such as
Rome Beauty, peeled, cored,
and diced

Combine the tamarind and boiling water in a bowl. Mash to break up the tamarind and set aside to soak at least 2 hours, or overnight.

Strain the tamarind into a large saucepan, pressing with the back of a spoon to extract all the liquid. Discard the solids. Stir in the honey and apples and place over medium-high heat. Bring to a boil, reduce to a simmer, cover, and cook, stirring occasionally, about 30 minutes, until the mixture resembles thick applesauce. Chill until serving time.

Makes 2 cups

orange bread with cranberry butter

This traditional, easy-to-make quick bread features oranges—a favorite Latin fruit. The only trick to light, delicious quick breads is not to overmix the ingredients, but just barely blend until the flour disappears.

½ cup (1 stick) unsalted butter, softened

1¼ cups sugar

2 large eggs

¾ cup buttermilk

grated zest of 2 oranges

½ cup freshly squeezed orange juice

1 teaspoon vanilla extract

3 cups sifted all-purpose flour

1½ teaspoons baking powder

1 teaspoon baking soda

1 teaspoon salt

confectioners' sugar, for dusting

Cranberry Butter, recipe follows, for serving

Preheat the oven to 350°F. Generously butter and flour a 9 × 5 × 3-inch loaf pan.

In a large bowl, cream the butter and sugar. Beat in the eggs one at a time. Add the buttermilk, orange zest, juice, and vanilla and beat until smooth.

In another bowl, stir together the flour, baking powder, baking soda, and salt. Add to the orange juice mixture and stir just until the flour disappears.

Spoon into the prepared pan, smoothing the top. Bake 45 to 55 minutes, until the sides shrink away from the pan and a toothpick inserted in the center comes out clean. Cool in the pan on a rack about 10 minutes, then invert to remove.

Dust with confectioners' sugar and serve warm, with the cranberry butter.

Makes 1 loaf

cranberry butter

¹/₂ cup dried cranberries

1 cup freshly squeezed orange juice

1 cup (2 sticks) unsalted butter, softened

5 tablespoons confectioners' sugar

In a small saucepan, combine the cranberries and orange juice and bring to a simmer over medium heat. Remove from the heat and let steep for 30 minutes.

Drain the cranberries and finely chop. Transfer to a bowl, add the butter and confectioners' sugar, and beat with a wooden spoon until completely combined. Scrape into small ramekins, or place on a sheet of heavy plastic wrap and roll into a cylinder. If necessary, chill to set. Remove from the refrigerator 15 minutes before serving to soften.

Makes about 1¹/₂ cups

buttermilk biscuits
with jalapeño jam

1 ³/₄ cups all-purpose flour

2 teaspoons baking powder

1 tablespoon sugar

¹/₂ teaspoon salt

¹/₂ cup (1 stick) unsalted
  butter

³/₄ cup buttermilk

Jalapeño Jam, recipe follows,
  for serving

Great biscuits with the added tang of buttermilk—one of Mary Sue's favorite ingredients—are always a treat. Try dabbing sweet-and-spicy jalapeño jam on grilled chops or roasted lamb in place of the old mint jelly standby.

Preheat the oven to 400°F.

In a large bowl, stir together the flour, baking powder, sugar, and salt. Using a pastry blender or your fingertips, cut in the butter until the mixture resembles coarse meal. Make a well in the center and pour in the milk all at once. Stir just until a shaggy dough is formed.

On a lightly floured board, gently knead the dough three or four times. Pat out the dough to a square about ¹/₂ inch thick. With a 3-inch round biscuit cutter or glass dipped in flour, cut out biscuits and transfer to an ungreased baking sheet. (You can also cut out squares with a sharp paring knife.) Bake 10 to 12 minutes, until golden brown. Serve hot with the jalapeño jam.

Makes about 6 biscuits

jalapeño jam

12 red or green jalapeño chiles, stemmed, seeded, and chopped

2 red bell peppers, cored, seeded, and chopped

6 serrano chiles, stemmed and seeded if desired

4 1/2 cups sugar

1 cup white vinegar

6 ounces liquid fruit pectin

In a blender or food processor, puree the jalapeños, bell peppers, and serranos until well chopped.

In a large saucepan, combine the chopped pepper mixture, the sugar, and the vinegar. Bring to a rolling boil and boil 10 minutes. Skim any foam from the top, then add the pectin and return to a boil for 1 minute. Cool and transfer to a crock and refrigerate.

Makes about 6 cups

spicy corn muffins with green chiles

1 tablespoon vegetable oil

12 serrano chiles

1 cup cornmeal

1 cup all-purpose flour

2 tablespoons sugar

2 teaspoons baking powder

1 teaspoon salt

$^1/_2$ teaspoon freshly ground black pepper

1 large egg, beaten

1 cup buttermilk or plain yogurt

6 tablespoons unsalted butter, melted, or vegetable oil

1 cup fresh or thawed frozen corn kernels

As these darling little muffins bake, thin green serrano chiles rise to the surface, poking out their hot little stems. But they are not as spicy as they sound, since eating the whole chile is optional.

Preheat the oven to 425°F. Butter a 12-cup muffin pan.

Heat the oil in a large skillet over high heat. Toss in the chiles and sear, turning, until evenly blackened. Drain on paper towels.

In a large bowl, mix together the cornmeal, flour, sugar, baking powder, salt, and pepper. Make a well in the center and add the egg, buttermilk, and melted butter. Whisking from the center, combine the ingredients into a loose, slightly lumpy batter. Fold in the corn.

Pour into the prepared muffin cups, filling them two-thirds full. Insert a chile in the center of each, stem end up, and bake 15 minutes, or until the muffins begin to pull away from the sides of the pan. Cool in the pan on a rack 10 minutes. Invert to remove, and serve warm or at room temperature.

Makes 12 muffins

café
de olla

4 cups water

4 ounces piloncillo (Mexican
    raw sugar cones) or ¹/₂ cup
    packed dark brown sugar

2 cinnamon sticks

¹/₂ teaspoon anise seeds

1 cup medium- to coarse-
    ground Viennese-roast
    coffee

2 cups low-fat milk

The first time we tasted classic spiced Mexican coffee, we were relaxing in the Puebla town square in the evening. All at once people started clinking their glasses with spoons to indicate they were ready for refills, and the waiter carefully filled their glasses. We like it at home for hearty winter brunches.

In a saucepan, combine the water, sugar, cinnamon, and anise seeds. Bring to a boil over medium heat, stirring to dissolve the sugar. Stir in the coffee, remove from the heat, cover, and let steep 5 minutes.

In a small saucepan, heat the milk over medium-high heat and carefully whisk until frothy. Strain the coffee through a fine sieve, pour into small cups, and serve immediately, with the frothed milk in a pitcher alongside.

Serves 6

cantaloupe liquado

2 1/2 cups chopped peeled
    cantaloupe (about 1 small)

1 1/2 cups cold milk

2 cups chopped ice

3 tablespoons honey

Blended fruit drinks are a great use for fruit that is overripe, or overabundant. These milk and fruit juice combinations are sold at juice stands all over Mexico.

    Combine the cantaloupe, milk, ice, and honey in a blender or food processor and puree until smooth. Pour into tall glasses and serve immediately.

Serves 4 to 6

hot tip

HOW TO KEEP AN EDGE

Knives are your most important tools in the kitchen. When you think about how often you use them and how much pleasure a good one can give, you will realize this is not the place to scrimp and save. There's no need to purchase a set of knives. Instead, buy three good ones—a 3- to 4-inch parer, a serrated blade, and a good 10- to 12-inch chef's knife. The blade on the chef's knife should be carbon steel or a combination of stainless and high-carbon steel, and it should go the whole length of the knife, from handle to tip. Carbon holds an edge the longest. At home, we use a 10-inch parer, and on the show and in the restaurant, we rely on our trusty Japanese carbon-steel blades made by Takayuki.

The key with any knife, of course, is to keep the original bevel on the edge by sharpening often. With a steel, swipe the entire length of the blade, at about a 15-degree angle, five or six times on each side every 10 minutes while cutting.

At some point, however, every knife loses its edge (since so many molecules get shaved off), and then you need to take it to a knife or cutlery store for professional sharpening. There the knife's edge can be restored with a tool known as a stone. For the knives we use at home, we like to do this close to holiday time, when our kitchens will be doing extra duty.

index

mary sue & her mom, ruth

susan & her mom, ruthie

susan & her mom, ruthie

mary sue & her mom, ruth